HORIZON

MARCH, 1963 · VOLUME V, NUMBER 4

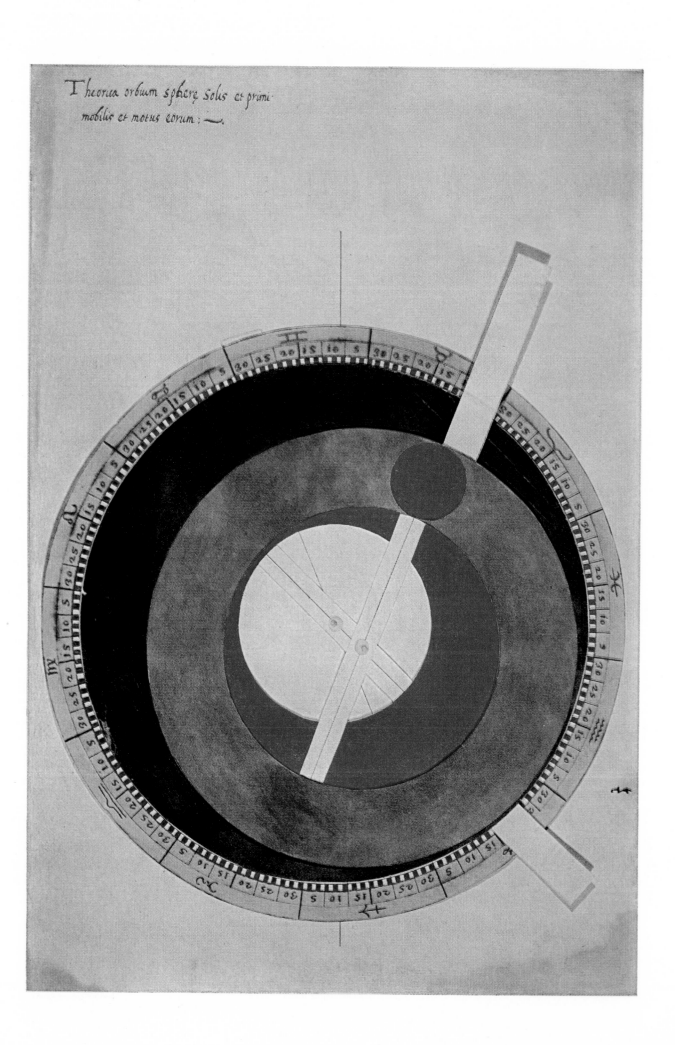

HORIZON
A Magazine of the Arts

MARCH, 1963 · VOLUME V, NUMBER 4

PUBLISHER
James Parton

EDITORIAL DIRECTOR
Joseph J. Thorndike. Jr.

EDITOR
William Harlan Hale
MANAGING EDITOR
Eric Larrabee
ASSOCIATE EDITOR
Ralph Backlund
ASSISTANT EDITORS
Ada Pesin
Jane Wilson
Albert Bermel
CONTRIBUTING EDITOR
Margery Darrell
EDITORIAL ASSISTANTS
Shirley Abbott, Caroline Backlund
Wendy Buehr, Priscilla Flood
COPY EDITOR
Mary Ann Pfeiffer
Assistants: Joan Rehe, Ruth H. Wolfe

ART DIRECTOR
Irwin Glusker
Associate Art Director: Elton Robinson

ADVISORY BOARD
Gilbert Highet, *Chairman*
Frederick Burkhardt   Oliver Jensen
Marshall B. Davidson   Jotham Johnson
Richard M. Ketchum   John Walker

EUROPEAN CONSULTING EDITOR
J. H. Plumb
Christ's College, Cambridge

EUROPEAN BUREAU
Gertrudis Feliu, *Chief*
11 rue du Bouloi, Paris

HORIZON is published every two months by American Heritage Publishing Co., Inc. Executive and editorial offices: 551 Fifth Ave., New York 17, N.Y. HORIZON welcomes contributions but can assume no responsibility for unsolicited material.

All correspondence about subscriptions should be addressed to: HORIZON Subscription Office, 379 West Center St., Marion, Ohio.

Single Copies: $4.50
Annual Subscriptions: $21.00 in the U.S. & Can.
$22.00 elsewhere

An annual index is published every September, priced at $1. HORIZON is also indexed in the *Readers Guide to Periodical Literature.*

Title registered U.S. Patent Office

Second-class postage paid at New York, N.Y., and at additional mailing offices.

COVER: This jeweled book cover is one of the many treasures of Venice originally commissioned for use in St. Mark's Cathedral. The book it was made to enclose has disappeared, the only clue to its contents being the portraits of Christ and of the apostles surrounding Him. Moreover, one of the apostles too has disappeared, to be inexplicably replaced by an angel, seen directly above Christ's head. The binding, which dates from the tenth century, is gilded silver; rows of pearls and semiprecious stones outline its borders and the enameled medallions, which depict the holy figures in Byzantine style. An article on the greatest treasure of the doges, Venice itself, begins on page 14.

FRONTISPIECE: Despite its startling resemblance to some recent manifestations in avant-garde art (see HORIZON for January, 1963, page 17), this elegant device in fact belongs far back in the rear guard. It is a sixteenth-century volvelle, a contrivance of heavy drawing paper designed to show the motion of the planets according to the then accepted Ptolemaic system. Thus, with its movable circles and pointers, it was a sort of two-dimensional planetarium. This is one of eleven such volvelles in a beautifully executed manuscript now in the possession of the New York rare-book firm of H. P. Kraus.

THE FIFTH

Four times it has achieved—and lost—a common

In April, 1944, at the dinner table of General Charles de Gaulle in Algiers, I heard my host remark, with characteristic finality: "Once the war is won, we shall certainly reunite Europe; that is to say, Western, democratic, and Christian Europe." Nineteen years later no seasoned visitor to what Winston Churchill called "this noble continent" can fail to note the fulfillment of the General's prophecy. The new European exudes self-confidence. What was once Europe's age-old pessimism about its ability to get along with itself has been replaced by an almost unbridled optimism. Moreover, the European now refers less often to French, German, or Italian ideas; he attributes them to Europe as a whole. This Europe is well on the way to becoming what can only be called a new country. Far from being resigned to "playing Greece to American Rome," it is dreaming of a greater future on its own.

Strangely enough, with all the attention that has been paid to Europe's emergent political and economic union, less emphasis has been put on its emergent psychological and cultural union. Its people have, in this, been ahead of its governments, moving to enter a common market of the mind while political unity still waits to be achieved. There is gradually coming to be something called a European personality, and this has come about—paradoxically—at the very time that the European governments have been renouncing their far-flung empires. The new European thinks in terms of an empire of the spirit, once more the center of mankind's intellectual and cultural development.

Here, and not in the field of economics, is the European miracle. And this re-emergence of a European avatar is the more remarkable because, as I count them, it is the fifth in a series—something no other area, unless it is China, can boast. In fact,

to appreciate what is happening in Europe today, it is important to recall those previous periods when, in one form or another, Europe has felt and thought as a single unit.

The first was, of course, ancient Rome.

After the battle of Zama, when Scipio finally defeated Hannibal, Rome started expanding in earnest. By the time Hadrian set limits to the empire, a state with a common language and a common citizenship embraced southern and western Europe, North Africa, and the Near East. What is more extraordinary, this empire's prestige was such that it inspired pride of belonging to it in men as diverse as Saint Paul the Jew and Alaric the Visigoth. Even after the Roman imperium had split into two parts under separate emperors, in the minds of men it still remained one and indivisible. Not Rome's fall itself could destroy the Western peoples' conception of the world they knew as a single entity.

Four centuries later the historical pattern recurred. Much as the Carthaginian invasion of Italy sparked the Roman expansion, so advancing Islam encouraged the formation of a great new Frankish kingdom. Charlemagne ruled from the Pyrenees to the Elbe River, from Hamburg to Rome—over roughly what is today the European Economic Community. As a physical fact, most of this kingdom was German, but its "secular theory" was Latin and ecclesiastical. Though it too divided, Carolingian Europe ultimately transformed itself into the Holy Roman Empire, which lasted formally from A.D. 962 until Napoleon Bonaparte usurped the imperial crown in 1806.

This international community of knights and theologians possessed a common religion, a common language, a common social structure, and it engaged in common action—no less than

Europa, beloved of Zeus in the guise of a bull, rides again as the symbol for an awakening continent.

EUROPE

culture. The new unity is also of the mind, and may endure   By EDGAR ANSEL MOWRER

nine Crusades! At its height, in the mid-thirteenth century, the University of Paris attracted scholars from all of Europe, among them Albertus Magnus from Germany, Bonaventura and Aquinas from Italy, and Roger Bacon from England. Students from whatever country felt completely at home.

Though again the sense of Europe as a single church-empire faded away, not long thereafter it revived, as an international community of poets, artists, musicians, and students of classical learning (the humanists) spread from Italy to the four corners of the Continent. The Europeans of the Renaissance, in a sort of Hegelian antithesis to the Age of Faith, rejected the church-empire's "otherworldliness" and, when the advancing Turks blocked access to the East, embarked upon those marvelous voyages of discovery that within four centuries enabled Europe—as a "little peninsula on the continent of Asia"—to make its power, influence, and eventually its scientific leadership world-wide.

During this period, though first Spain (and later, France) made unsuccessful attempts at European political unity, disruptive forces emerged once more in the Reformation, the Counter Reformation, and the wars of religion and dynastic succession. The "Third Europe" was torn to shreds. Yet out of these failures to unite came the "Fourth Europe" of the Enlightenment.

"During the first two-thirds of the eighteenth century," writes Harold Nicolson, "culture was more international or cosmopolitan than it had ever been since the Middle Ages. Writers, artists, and thinkers did not regard themselves as the natives of any particular country. They looked upon themselves as citizens of what they called the Republic of Letters." And they spread their international outlook to many contemporary rulers, already cosmopolitan by marriage. Louis XV of France had a Polish wife.

In Britain the Georges were more German than English. Frederick the Great of Prussia spoke French at the court of Potsdam and more or less despised his German subjects.

Soon, perhaps logically, the Republic of Letters succumbed to its own children, those American and French revolutions which, in turn, were carrying the cult of reason and equality farther abroad in the world. Napoleon's almost successful efforts to impose French rule on Europe stimulated intense patriotic feelings in multitudes who had felt little or none before. At the last minute, in 1821, the principal members of the Holy Alliance— Russia, Prussia, and Austria—made an attempt to preserve unity by issuing the Protocol of Troppau, which would have turned Europe into a confederation under the control of a single Diet of Great Powers empowered to regulate the internal politics of member states, thereby ending national sovereignty. After their failure little of the Enlightenment's cosmopolitanism survived. Europe entered on a century of unbridled nationalism, culminating—one is tempted to say, inevitably—in the two world wars that cost the European countries their overseas empires, their political and military predominance, and all but their very existence.

It must be said of Europe's recurrent efforts toward unity, despite their failure, that each represented a surge of creative energy and was often enough accompanied by a corresponding period of fruitful activity in the arts. Moreover, the dream of a single Europe persisted. Even in the high tide of nationalism in the decades before World War I, a powerful current toward unification could still be felt. For one thing, many then believed that national conflicts were a thing of the past. In the years before 1914, while the Great Powers were drifting toward dis-

5

*Roman Europe was the first
to be united, in a single language and law,
proudly shared by diverse peoples.*

pean dream, both intellectual and political, of great earnestness and appeal, though once again it was to be undone by harsh realities. Whatever else one may say of the years after World War I, they did see man's first attempt to create a world authority, the League of Nations, and (in 1928) that supreme effort in human futility, the Kellogg-Briand Pact "outlawing war." It was then that the Austrian Robert Coudenhove-Kalergi founded a Pan-European Union, and Alexandr Stamboliski and Aristide Briand urged conciliation and bade Europe's peoples to "learn to speak European." Going further, in his remarkable book *The Revolt of the Masses,* the Spanish philosopher Ortega y Gasset wrote boldly that not the single countries but the "unity of Europe" was the reality. Some, like Thomas Mann, agreed. But the possibility of an intellectual *rapprochement*—between French and Germans, for example—was never enough as long as the economic, political, and (for lack of a better word) psychological base to build it on was lacking. It was for this that we had to wait until after World War II, and it is this which distinguishes the present "revival" from the earlier ones.

When the war was indeed over, the prospects for a European future seemed dark. The victorious British were exhausted. The Germans lay stunned under the magnitude of their incomprehensible defeat. The half-defeated French emerged apathetic and apolitical. Once again the victors reacted to the horror of the conflict by attempting to establish a world order, this time in the form of the United Nations. But it was cold comfort for Europe. For while the U.N. plus American power might protect them against war and communism, it could not restore them to the leadership they had previously enjoyed and still obscurely felt they deserved.

For a few years their situation seemed hopeless. Yet in the ruins, almost imperceptibly, something was stirring that was in time to produce the "Fifth Europe"; it was the people's recognition that their misery was their own fault, the logical result of two irresponsible "civil wars." As the Europeans gradually emerged from the shock of war, they found themselves unwilling to die, reluctant either to submit to Russia or to remain perpetually the "objects" of America's avuncular guidance, however well-intentioned. And at this point they produced a number of leaders who insisted in and out of season that the separate peoples must seek for themselves what no one had ever been able to impose on them by force—namely, unity.

France, defeated in 1940, seems to have been the first to react. In Bordeaux, in June, 1940, I remember hearing French conservatives, who were later to support Vichy, justify their acceptance of the armistice by arguing that a German victory would put a stop to the endless Franco-German feud. Paradoxically it has been France, perhaps the first European country to develop a sense of nationality, which has over the years produced the greatest number of pan-European prophets. Pierre Dubois, in the fourteenth century, advocated a union of Christian princes against the Turks; Maximilien de Béthune, Duke of Sully, as Minister to King Henry IV evolved a "Grand De-

aster, Europe enjoyed individual freedom and the illusion of permanent peace. Outside of "barbarous" Russia and Turkey, men and women traveled where they would, without passports or frontier difficulties. Civilization, many Europeans thought, had done away with the possibility of major war.

This was the spirit behind the founding of the Hague Court in 1899. It produced in 1910 Norman Angell's book *The Great Illusion* (which had an enormous influence on young people like me), "demonstrating" that war had become too expensive to be practical. It inspired the efforts of the American sculptor Hendrick Christian Andersen to create plans for a "world city of communication" and those of his co-worker, the Italian judge Gaetano Meale (whose pen name was Umano), to produce a really practical plan for world government. Socialists like Shaw and Wells in England, artists like Romain Rolland in France (whose ten-volume French novel, *Jean Christophe,* appeared between 1904 and 1912 and had a *German* as hero), labored mightily for international reconciliation.

Such hopes and expectations—and those much like them that were to follow in the twenties and thirties—were of course doomed to disappointment. They remained the preoccupation of intellectuals and a few politicians, all too easily overturned by the onrush of events. Before 1914 men like Emile Verhaeren, the Belgian poet, could dream of reconciling *"la France ardente et la grave Allemagne."* But the outbreak of the war plunged these idealists into a bitterness from which they never recovered and ultimately led Rolland and others to support Soviet communism, under the impression (as I heard him remark in 1937) that it was "the last refuge of humanity."

The period between the wars witnessed a revival of the Euro-

*Medieval Europe carried on the
memory, in a common church, common customs,
and a common cause—the Crusades.*

sign" for the creation of a Christian Republic of European Nations; Bernardin de St.-Pierre, author of the novel *Paul et Virginie,* proposed an association of European states to guarantee perpetual peace; and in the nineteenth century Saint-Simon the utopian and Thierry the politician were followed by Victor Hugo the writer, who in 1859 predicted that the "United States of Europe will crown the Old World just as the United States of America crowns the New." Now, in the 1940's, France produced Jean Monnet, the "Mr. Europe" of our generation, and the Schuman Plan, the coal-and-steel community on which the Fifth Europe would be built.

The situation today, less than twenty years after what seemed Europe's death agony, was described to me by a Belgian diplomat. "The six original members of the European Economic Community have now scrambled themselves far too successfully ever to unscramble themselves," he said. "Give us ten years more and nearly all will think, feel, and act European as a matter of course."

How has this come about? There are, it seems to me, three ways that Europeans have arrived at their new sense of identity: by conviction, by calculation, and without quite knowing it. The first group includes certain of the older leaders, but the majority are young, those who were soldiers in the last war or as children were indelibly marked by it, or those who have known only the postwar world—that is, today's youth. A poll of French young people from sixteen to twenty-four years of age, in the summer of 1962, revealed that only 5 per cent opposed European unity while 58 per cent were convinced that Europe would become a "Third Force" equal to the U.S.A. and the U.S.S.R.

Most older citizens are, however, European only by calculation. They accept some degree of economic and political unification (not too much or too fast) because the alternative seems to be impotent poverty. At heart they remain nation-minded and think in terms of nationality. One such, as he himself has made clear, is Charles de Gaulle. His mind recognizes that Europe had to unite to survive and become a "dike of power and prosperity of the same order as the United States." To that end, the reconciliation of France with Germany was essential. But his heart remains attached to French "greatness" and a "Europe of Fatherlands."

Another group of Europeans-by-calculation are the workmen. The Common Market has brought them an undreamed-of prosperity and, in most places, overemployment. Already, more than a million people are working outside their own countries, and by 1969 all obstacles to the free movement of labor will have disappeared. To them the new Europe means the first taste of what Americans have long taken for granted—in short, what President Truman called "the good things of life."

Finally, millions within and without the Common Market are Europeans without knowing it. Increasingly their common folkways—radio and television programs, books, clothing, food—are creating more similar mental and emotional patterns than those who adopt them may realize.

While the Europeans-by-calculation have made the Economic Community prosperous, the Europeans-by-conviction have more importantly been laying the foundation of a new European culture. They have begun it chiefly at the bottom—in education. From the founding of the first Maison d'Europe at Douai in 1948, centers of Europeanism have multiplied. A pamphlet entitled "The European Guide to Teaching," published in 1958 by the European Culture Center of Lausanne, devotes three full pages to "good European addresses": in addition to official organizations, the Guide lists no less than ten popular movements, three cultural foundations, ten associations and specialized centers, and twenty publications.

The first European school at Luxembourg was founded in 1952 with seventy-two pupils. In 1957 it was taken over by the six governments of the European Coal and Steel Community. By 1960–61 it had nine hundred ten pupils. Three more such schools have been created, at Brussels and Mol/Geel in Belgium, and at Ispra-Varese in Italy. Each of these institutions will soon be empowered to grant baccalaureate diplomas, admitting their students to any university within the Common Market countries.

The aim of the teachers is specific: "Sharing the same games, grouped in common classes, boys and girls of various languages and nationalities will learn to know and value each other and to live together . . . becoming in spirit Europeans well prepared to complete and consolidate the task undertaken by their fathers of consolidating a prosperous and united Europe."

At the university level Europe's professors—with some American help—have brought into being no less than eighteen institutes of European studies, as well as the College of Europe at Bruges. As far back as 1955, at Messina, the six Common

*Europe in the Renaissance
extended its explosive energies into natural
science and the voyages of discovery.*

Market governments agreed that one of the first three institutions to be created was a university of Europe. They confirmed this idea in the Euratom Treaty of 1957 and, at the Bonn meeting in 1961, decided to locate such a university at Florence and to open its doors to students in the autumn of 1962.

Yet the university that was supposed to crown Europe's education pyramid still stands empty. For a debate has arisen between those who emphasize the new Europe's need for ever more teachers and professors with a "European vocation" and those, including many professors and the French government, who believe that existing universities can in time fill the need. Instead of a new university they would create a European research center where specialists in the various aspects of European unity would train an educational elite to carry on the idea.

Another big spoon stirring the European melting pot is the growing army of exchange students between the various countries. In part they are encouraged by governments; in part by organizations like the *Union National des Etudiants Français* or the *Deutsche Studentenschaft* and by international youth congresses; in part by families making deliberate sacrifices in order that their children may spend time abroad. Increasing cooperation among all manner of professional people is also having its effect. Today there is, so to speak, only one "school" of painting in all free Europe, and few are the artists who can be parochial and content. Several European governments have agreed to build an international "artists' city" in Paris, with hundreds of studios and workshops. In 1962 the Council of Europe organized in Vienna the latest of its exhibitions of European art, entitled "Circa 1400" and demonstrating that art styles have often ignored national borders.

A million and more workers, as we have noted, have found jobs outside their own countries. German domestic servants, increasingly rare at home, readily respond to the offer of employment in England; Dutch girls are eager to go as maids to Germany. The results are sometimes bewildering. In Frankfurt I was unable to get my breakfast at the hotel until another waiter explained that the one to whom I had given my order did not understand German! A shift to Italian brought prompt action.

Vacations abroad are further spreading the European gospel. Millions now spend their holidays touring in some other European country than their own, a large percentage of them in buses or automobiles. Winter vacations on the coast of Spain have become so common in England that "Costa Brava" is a part of the language, and crops up frequently in the captions to *Punch* cartoons. Some three hundred thousand Swedes visit Italy each year, many in their own cars. The Germans are everywhere. When rich they seem to regard a house in Switzerland or an island off the coast of Spain as a necessary status symbol—or, at least, as a tax loss. Italians, with their snorting motor scooters, invade France and Switzerland each summer. Even the French, who formerly tended to scorn foreign travel since everything was "better in France," now vacation in Germany, Switzerland, and even Scandinavia. A little watchmaker in Paris, an old friend of mine, last summer went off with his wife and twenty other Parisians to spend the holiday *walking* through the Black Forest in Germany.

Inside the Common Market any sort of identity card serves as a passport, and the gradual reduction of tariff barriers is not only increasing and improving consumption but bringing about ever greater uniformity of taste. Take food: the Germans are eating more French cheeses and drinking more French wines; so are Scandinavians; almost any Paris café serves Munich beer. For some mysterious reason the entire Continent inclines less to its own brand of strong drink than to Scotch whisky. Italians are eating more meat, both because they can afford it and because of the growing repugnance to corpulence. As a result even such famous *fettuccine* palaces as Alfredo's in Rome no longer serve a heaped-up plate of pasta as an entire meal. And all of Europe eats Belgian vegetables.

The broadening exchange of goods is also bringing about greater uniformity in housing and in clothing. The cheapest and best technical appliances, dishes, pottery, and textiles, regardless of origin, are spreading everywhere. So, amazingly, are clothes. Today the external marks of class and nationality are disappearing among Europe's women. At the 1961 Congress of the German Social Democratic Party in Cologne, a new stylishness was evident among women politicians and politicians' wives who, as late as the Weimar Republic, would have exulted in their dowdiness. Today's German women are being exhorted by every medium from television to newspaper ads to exchange their former "sober decency" for *"dezente Eleganz,"* and to "cultivate their legs" by wearing thin nylons. More and more of them do both.

Europe in the Age of Reason became a cosmopolitan community with its first allegiance to the "Republic of Letters."

All very well, some people may object, but a Common Market, common fashions, even a common way of life, does not necessarily create an original culture. For that something more is necessary—if not a common philosophy, at least a common artistic and intellectual style. Is Europe producing it? Here it is interesting to note that the first half of the twentieth century was sharply characterized by the individual artist's and thinker's reaction to a prevailing "disorder" in the world. It is certainly no coincidence that two agnostic and depressing philosophies emerged after World War I, in Viennese logical positivism and German existentialism, one of which simply denied the validity of metaphysics, while the other affirmed man's incurably lamentable state by describing human life as essentially "absurd." To the dispirited French of 1945, this seemed only too true, and the result was a spate of existentialist plays and novels. Once the Europeans began to recover their self-respect, however, life began to appear less "absurd" and individuals somewhat less abject. As a philosophical influence, certainly existentialism began to decline around 1955, and many predict that the type of literature it inspired will not last much longer.

Something similar may also be happening in the arts, though whether the new optimism will affect abstract painting and atonal music remains to be seen. Their early practitioners, at any event, back in the years before the First World War, steadfastly maintained that the destruction of accepted art forms reflected not only a need for renewal but the disintegration of man's inner life. The established values had then been thoroughly disrupted, but have they now been restored? Whether they have or not, if the New Europe does discover common values or revives old ones in a new form, it is tempting to think that music and art might move toward some sort of stability and order—toward, in short, a new classicism.

In forming a new cultural image of itself Europe also has the advantage of its long and deep traditions. Certainly it is no accident that in a symposium in August and September of 1962 a group of eminent Europeans agreed that what distinguished contemporary Europe from both the United States and the Soviet Union was Europe's unshakable faith in the individual, whether as hero, saint, or martyr. Both America and Russia, according to Denis de Rougemont, wish to eliminate diversity and tensions in favor of a smoothly working organization. Europe, on the other hand, knows the value of diversity, of contradiction, of permanent criticism, and of a certain "equilibrium resulting from innumerable tensions." Arthur Koestler credits Europe alone with a sense of continuity in change; Asia, he thinks, has continuity without change, and America and Australia change without continuity.

What remains to be seen is whether or not Europe can find a way to preserve its traditional values—values based, at least in part, on rigid class distinctions and privileges—in a democratizing world where privilege has become precarious. The new Europe must not become, as a number of British intellectuals seem to fear it will, a rich white man's club in superior isolation from its former colonies in Asia and Africa. There are bound to be losses. The rich diversity of Europe, with its innumerable local differences in taste and temper, is not likely to survive untouched when a "common cake of custom" covers all. Can Europe have both *Corton Charlemagne* and Coca-Cola? Neither we nor they know, but what can safely be said is that the question is now once again open to argument, where for a time it seemed totally overshadowed by the looming mass societies of America and Russia. What Europe is defiantly asserting is what, at war's end, it seemed so clearly to have lost—and that is, its relevance to the future.

Any modern Western culture is of course bound to be in part world-wide, the result of the spread of (essentially Western) ideas, styles, and techniques to the entire globe. In part it will be Atlantic, for the "Americanization" of Europe has gone much too far to be undone. Only in spirit can it be specifically European. But this spirit is precisely what the Fifth Europe wishes most to develop. And whether we like or not, this Fifth Europe is—short of general catastrophe—here to stay. We on our side of the Atlantic can ignore it, oppose it, or come to terms with it. For today the people of what was once the Old Country are very much on their own, and enjoying the feeling hugely. They will be gratified if we choose to co-operate with them on equal terms but not heartbroken if we decide otherwise. My guess is that we shall have to run very fast to keep up.

Edgar Ansel Mowrer began his career as a foreign correspondent in World War I, and a collection of his dispatches, Germany Puts the Clock Back, *won the Pulitzer Prize in 1933.*

By GILBERT HIGHET

Diogenes has a snug wooden barrel and Alexander a surprisingly gray beard for one so young (he was only twenty) in this version of their encounter from

BEGINNING A NEW SERIES: *History has reached some of its high moments of drama as well as human comedy in significant meetings between contrasting and memorable persons. In subsequent issues, among other encounters, that of Attila and Pope Leo the Great will be recalled by C. V. Wedgwood; that of Mary Queen of Scots and John Knox, by H. R. Trevor-Roper; that of Napoleon and Czar Alexander on a raft at Tilsit, by J. Christopher Herold.*

10

THE DOG HAS HIS DAY

a fifteenth-century French manuscript

Lying on the bare earth, shoeless, bearded, half-naked, he looked like a beggar or a lunatic. He was one, but not the other. He had opened his eyes with the sun at dawn, scratched, done his business like a dog at the roadside, washed at the public fountain, begged a piece of breakfast bread and a few olives, eaten them squatting on the ground, and washed them down with a few handfuls of water scooped from the spring. (Long ago he had owned a rough wooden cup, but he threw it away when he saw a boy drinking out of his hollowed hands.) Having no work to go to and no family to provide for, he was free. As the market place filled up with shoppers and merchants and gossipers and sharpers and slaves and foreigners, he had strolled through it for an hour or two. Everybody knew him, or knew of him. They would throw sharp questions at him, and get sharper answers. Sometimes they threw jeers, and got jibes; sometimes bits of food, and got scant thanks; sometimes a mischievous pebble, and got a shower of stones and abuse. They were not quite sure whether he was mad or not. He knew they were mad, all mad, each in a different way; they amused him. Now he was back at his home.

It was not a house, not even a squatter's hut. He thought everybody lived far too elaborately, expensively, anxiously. What good is a house? No one needs privacy: natural acts are not shameful; we all do the same things, and need not hide them. No one needs beds and chairs and such furniture: the animals live healthy lives and sleep on the ground. All we require, since nature did not dress us properly, is one garment to keep us warm, and some shelter from rain and wind. So he had one blanket—to dress him in the daytime and cover him at night—and he slept in a cask. His name was Diogenes. He was the founder of the creed called Cynicism (the word means "doggishness"); he spent much of his life in the rich, lazy, corrupt Greek city of Corinth, mocking and satirizing its people, and occasionally converting one of them.

His home was not a barrel made of wood: too expensive. It was a storage jar made of earthenware, something like a modern fuel tank—no doubt discarded because a break had made it useless. He was not the first to inhabit such a thing: the refugees driven into Athens by the Spartan invasion had been forced to sleep in casks. But he was the first who ever did so by choice, out of principle.

Diogenes was not a degenerate or a maniac. He was a philosopher who wrote plays and poems and essays expounding his doctrine; he talked to those who cared to listen; he had pupils who admired him. But he taught chiefly by example. All should live naturally, he said, for what is natural is normal and cannot possibly be evil or shameful. Live without conventions, which are artificial and false; escape complexities and superfluities and extravagances: only so can you live a free life. The rich man believes he possesses his big house with its many rooms and its elaborate furniture, his pictures and his expensive clothes, his horses and his servants and his bank accounts. He does not. He depends on them, he worries about them, he spends most of his life's energy looking after them; the thought of losing them makes him sick with anxiety. They possess him. He is their slave. In order to procure a quantity of false, perishable goods he has sold the only true, lasting good, his own independence.

There have been many men who grew tired of human society with its complications, and went away to live simply—on a small farm, in a quiet village, in a hermit's cave, or in the darkness of anonymity. Not so Diogenes. He was not a recluse, or a stylite, or a beatnik. He was a missionary. His life's aim was clear to him: it was "to restamp the currency." (He and his father had once been convicted for counterfeiting, long before he turned to philosophy, and this phrase was Diogenes' bold, unembarrassed joke on the subject.) To restamp the currency: to take the clean metal of human life, to erase the old false conventional markings, and to imprint it with its true values.

The other great philosophers of the fourth century before Christ taught mainly their own private pupils. In the shady groves and cool sanctuaries of the Academy, Plato discoursed to a chosen few on the unreality of this contingent existence. Aristotle, among the books and instruments and specimens and archives and research-workers of his Lyceum, pursued investigations and gave lectures that were rightly named *esoteric*, "for those within the walls." But for Diogenes, laboratory and specimens and lecture halls and pupils were all to be found in a crowd of ordinary people. Therefore he chose to live in Athens or in the rich city of Corinth, where travelers from all over the Mediterranean world constantly came and went. And, by design, he publicly behaved in such ways as to show people what real life was. He would constantly take up their spiritual coin, ring it on a stone, and laugh at its false superscription.

He thought most people were only half-alive, most men only half-men. At bright noonday he walked through the market place carrying a lighted lamp and inspecting the face of everyone he met. They asked him why. Diogenes answered, "I am trying to find a *man*."

To a gentleman whose servant was putting on his shoes for him, Diogenes said, "You won't be really happy until he wipes your nose for you: that will come after you lose the use of your hands."

Once there was a war scare so serious that it stirred even the lazy, profit-happy Corinthians. They began to drill, clean their weapons, and rebuild their neglected fortifications. Diogenes took his old cask and began to roll it up and down, back and forward. "When you are all so busy," he said, "I felt I ought to do *something*!"

nd so he lived—like a dog, some said, because he cared nothing for privacy and other human conventions, and because he showed his teeth and barked at those whom he disliked. Now he was lying in the sunlight, as contented as a dog on the warm ground, happier (he himself used to boast) than the Shah of Persia. Although he knew he was going to have an important visitor, he would not move.

The little square began to fill with people. Page boys elegantly dressed, spearmen speaking a rough foreign dialect, discreet secretaries, hard-browed officers, suave diplomats, they all gradually formed a circle centered on Diogenes. He looked them over, as a sober man looks at a crowd of tottering drunks, and shook his head. He knew who they were. They were the attendants of the conqueror of Greece, the servants of Alexander, the Macedonian king, who was visiting his newly subdued realm.

Only twenty, Alexander was far older and wiser than his years. Like all Macedonians he loved drinking, but he could usually handle it; and toward women he was nobly restrained and chivalrous. Like all Macedonians he loved fighting; he was a magnificent commander, but he was not merely a military automaton. He could think. At thirteen he had become a pupil of the greatest mind in Greece, Aristotle. No exact record of his schooling survives. It is clear, though, that Aristotle took the passionate, half-barbarous boy and gave him the best of Greek culture. He taught Alexander poetry: the young prince slept with the *Iliad* under his pillow and longed to emulate Achilles, who brought the mighty power of Asia to ruin. He taught him philosophy, in particular the shapes and uses of political power: a few years later Alexander was to create a supranational empire that was not merely a power system but a vehicle for the exchange of Greek and Middle Eastern cultures.

Aristotle taught him the principles of scientific research: during his invasion of the Persian domains Alexander took with him a large corps of scientists, and shipped hundreds of zoological specimens back to Greece for study. Indeed, it was from Aristotle that Alexander learned to seek out everything strange which might be instructive. Jugglers and stunt artists and virtuosos of the absurd he dismissed with a shrug; but on reaching India he was to spend hours discussing the problems of life and death with naked Hindu mystics, and later to see one demonstrate Yoga self-command by burning himself impassively to death.

ow, Alexander was in Corinth to take command of the League of Greek States which, after conquering them, his father Philip had created as a disguise for the New Macedonian Order. He was welcomed and honored and flattered. He was the man of the hour, of the century: he was unanimously appointed commander-in-chief of a new expedition against old, rich, corrupt Asia. Nearly everyone crowded to Corinth in order to congratulate him, to seek employment with him, even simply to see him: soldiers and statesmen, artists and merchants, poets and philosophers. He received their compliments graciously. Only Diogenes, although he lived in Corinth, did not visit the new monarch. With that generosity which Aristotle had taught him was a quality of the truly magnanimous man, Alexander determined to call upon Diogenes. Surely Dio-genes, the God-born, would acknowledge the conqueror's power by some gift of hoarded wisdom.

With his handsome face, his fiery glance, his strong supple body, his purple and gold cloak, and his air of destiny, he moved through the parting crowd, toward the Dog's kennel. When a king approaches, all rise in respect. Diogenes did not rise, he merely sat up on one elbow. When a monarch enters a precinct, all greet him with a bow or an acclamation. Diogenes said nothing.

There was a silence. Some years later Alexander speared his best friend to the wall, for objecting to the exaggerated honors paid to His Majesty; but now he was still young and civil. He spoke first, with a kindly greeting. Looking at the poor broken cask, the single ragged garment, and the rough figure lying on the ground, he said, "Is there anything I can do for you, Diogenes?"

"Yes," said the Dog. "Stand to one side. You're blocking the sunlight."

There was silence, not the ominous silence preceding a burst of fury, but a hush of amazement. Slowly, Alexander turned away. A titter broke out from the elegant Greeks, who were already beginning to make jokes about the Cur that looked at the King. The Macedonian officers, after deciding that Diogenes was not worth the trouble of kicking, were starting to guffaw and nudge one another. Alexander was still silent. To those nearest him he said quietly, "If I were not Alexander, I should be Diogenes." They took it as a paradox, designed to close the awkward little scene with a polite curtain line. But Alexander meant it. He understood Cynicism as the others could not. Later he took one of Diogenes' pupils with him to India as a philosophical interpreter (it was he who spoke to the naked *saddhus*). He was what Diogenes called himself, a *cosmopolitēs*, "citizen of the world." Like Diogenes, he admired the heroic figure of Hercules, the mighty conqueror who labors to help mankind while all others toil and sweat only for themselves. He knew that of all men then alive in the world only Alexander the conqueror and Diogenes the beggar were truly free.

BY VENICE

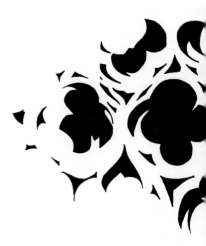

As one beguiled Frenchman put it, "She casts about you a charm as tender as the

Of all the cities of the earth, unquestionably the most hackneyed is Venice. Everybody who writes has written about her, or so it sometimes seems, from the myriad middle-aged ladylike aesthetes of the early 1900's to those many hardened professionals who earn an annual stipend by churning out their stock Venetian eulogy for the tourist season. Everyone who knows a paintbrush from a Pogo stick has painted the place, from Winston Churchill, the last of the doges, to the uncountable less distinguished enthusiasts whose sludgy prospects of the Salute may be inspected in almost any antique shop in almost any capital, tucked away between the tobacconist's wooden Indian and the candle snuffers. The Venetian legend has been debunked, of course, by casual scoffers as by dedicated rationalists; but in the end even the most sophisticated skeptic, breathing a pinched sigh of frustration, generally has to admit that all in all, notwithstanding, nevertheless, it is an undeniably fascinating place.

The road to St. Mark's has been trodden, down the centuries, by endless lines of eminent pilgrims, pressing toward that distant glitter as fervently as ever the knights pursued the Holy Grail. The mysteries of Venice have been enshrined by visiting celebrants as wildly disparate as Goethe and Henry James, Proust and Hans Andersen, Dickens and Hemingway, Dante and Disraeli, Ouida and Rousseau, Miss Mary McCarthy and Mrs. Humphry Ward, Shelley, Petrarch, Longfellow, George Sand and George Eliot—whose husband once made his own obeisance to the city by falling plumb out of his hotel window into the Grand Canal. Foreign painters of every school have painted famous pictures of the place, from Dürer by way of Turner's gorgeous fantasies to the brilliant splurge of Kokoschka—and who does not know the cloudy obscurantism of Great-aunt Agatha's water color above the mantelpiece in the spare room, *A Spring Dawn Over San Giorgio, Done During A Visit with Dear Henry, March 1887*?

"If I search for a synonym for music," wrote Nietzsche, in between his searches for Superman, "I find always and only Venice." Hitler also adored the place: he much admired the Doge's Palace, which would indeed have suited his temperament well; and according to legend he was seen one morning, during an official visit, ranging the quayside by himself in the small hours at a queer, crazed jog trot. Garibaldi was fond of the Doge's Palace, too: he thought he recognized himself in the figure of a particularly heroic commander in Vincentino's *Battle of Lepanto.*

No city has been more relentlessly gushed over, slushed through, daubed in purple prose, or ornamented with pink scented ribbon in maidenly diaries. It is with an effortless regality, though, that Venice rises above her adulations, for she is, as John Addington Symonds once remarked, a Shakespeare

POSSESSED

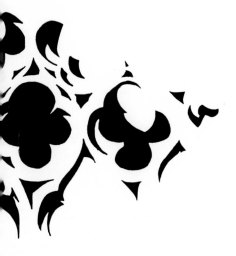

charm of woman. Other cities have admirers, Venice alone has lovers" By JAMES MORRIS

among cities—or perhaps, not to mix our cultures, a Giorgione. She is something different in kind, divinely or mystically infused, standing upon an opaline rung of her own among the civic hierarchies. Nobody, indeed, could call her faultless. She often stinks, she often grabs, she sometimes seems no more than one big vulgarized museum—a sort of feverish Williamsburg. Her winter climate is dank and drizzly. Her architecture, if you stand back, put down your wine glass, and look at her buildings with detachment, often turns out to be a hodgepodge of the sham and the mediocre.

Most people dislike *something* about Venice, if only the food or the hotel bill. Herbert Spencer the philosopher loathed the tessellations of the Doge's Palace ("the vertebral spine of a fish"). John Evelyn the diarist disliked the interior of the Basilica ("dim and dismal") and Mark Twain the exterior ("a vast and warty bug taking a meditative walk"). Ruskin particularly detested the church of San Giorgio Maggiore ("it is impossible to conceive a design more gross, more barbarous, more childish in conception, more servile in plagiarism, more insipid in result, more contemptible under every point of rational regard"). Charlie Chaplin took an instant dislike to the figures that embellish the Sansovino Library in the Piazzetta. D. H. Lawrence took an instant dislike to the place as a whole —"an abhorrent, green, slippery city." Most of us have felt

our moments of exasperation in Venice, and if we do not find her abhorrent exactly, or even very green, we know just what he meant about the slipperiness.

And yet when the parts are put together, the protrusions ironed out, Venice remains the perpetual siren. Bored to death with the very sound of the city, we still surreptitiously trail her glory through the travel pages of the women's magazines, still travel a thousand miles to spend our nightmarish weekends among her familiar splendors, still think of her with a certain breathless tremor of expectancy, as you might pay attention to an incipient miracle. She leaves you with an altered taste in your mouth—to some acrid, to others rose-sweet, as though she has arranged some slight alchemical change in your blood stream. The images she summons to mind are always sensual, and often actually sexual—for she is among the sexiest of cities. As one nineteenth-century Frenchman found, "Venice casts about you a charm as tender as the charm of woman. Other cities have admirers, Venice alone has lovers." In the seventeenth century the English traveler James Howell reached the conclusion that anyone who got to know Venice must "quickly make love to her"; two hundred years later Elizabeth Barrett Browning was in no less rapturous thrall when she wrote that "nothing is like it, nothing equal to it, not a second Venice in the world."

One is enough, perhaps; but even today, through the throb of the motorboats on the Grand Canal, through the singsong chatter of the guides, above the tinsel and the degradation of tourism, the music of Venice still sounds with a clear libidinous allure. You must shut your eyes to hear it properly, and lean out of your window into the damp sunshine, and presently you will catch it faintly, beyond the gentle tread of a liner's turning propellers, beyond the distant roar of the Adriatic surf on the beaches of Byron's Lido—the same lush tantalizing melody that has lured so many travelers to this shore, however conscientiously they stuffed their ears with wax or had themselves lashed to the door handles of the *wagon-lit*.

Why this siren song still captures us is a riddle of Venice. Men of all kinds have felt its strange compulsion, and women too, even those who have endured great sadness in the place or have been repelled by its combination of the crookbacked and the gorgeous. Venice is not a frank city. Her origins have been blurred by time, her purpose is meshed with contradictions, and her future is anybody's guess. You leave her enthralled indeed, but puzzled—half-relieved, half-regretful, and not quite sure what happened.

The key to her enigma is partly, I think, the organic shape of her. Corbusier called her "an object lesson for town planners," and she does form a neat, tight, symmetrical whole, lying there in the middle of her oozy lagoon as scrunched and commanding as the speckled spider at the hub of his web. The diverse sections of the city, itself an assemblage of islands, have been run together and diffused, linked by countless tacklike bridges —with the canals and alleyways like veins upon her skin and the mottled roof tops covering all like freckles. The opposing styles of her architecture, drawn from East and West, Gothic severity or Renaissance flare, have long since melted into one another, fused in old intimacy, so that the ancient Byzantine cathedral of Torcello stands symbolically on the frontier between the ribs and vaults of Western Europe and the bulbous domes of the East. Ruskin called the Doge's Palace the central edifice of the world, and everything about Venice still feels foursquare and metropolitan. Her images are slick, elegant, instantly recognizable: winged lions, campaniles, great golden horses, the long black lopsided silhouette of the gondola paddling silently out of the twilight. Venice, for so many generations the greatest of the trading powers, still feels like the shell of some great corporation, where the computers may no longer click and the sales graphs have been discarded, but where all the effulgent emblems of capitalism survive, glittering, purposeful, always functional.

Color, light, vivid space, contribute no less to the beguilement—colors often brash and intrusive, like advertising posters; colors sometimes moist and misty, when the sun rises over the dank, reedy lagoon and you see its sphere rising through a miasma of marsh vapors. Chiaroscuro was the forte of the Venetian masters, and this is still a ravishingly iridescent city. The best Venetian sunsets are rich and romantic. The best Venetian noondays are an exquisite, scintillating baby-blue. The best Venetian festivals are, to this day, events of dazzling

TEXT CONTINUED ON PAGE 25

16

The Stones of Venice

A PORTFOLIO BY ALEXANDER LIBERMAN

For more than eight hundred years the doges of Venice, as ostentatious and acquisitive as they were mighty, busily surrounded themselves with all that was beautiful. The Doge's Palace is itself a dazzling landmark and show place; the city as a whole is an illustrated history of Italian architecture. On the following eight pages HORIZON presents a portfolio in gravure of views of Venice by Alexander Liberman, the distinguished photographer, painter, and Editorial Director of Condé Nast publications.

The famous Basilica of St. Mark, shown on the opposite page as seen from the Piazza, was begun in the ninth century to house remains of the Saint, which had been brought to Venice from Alexandria by two enterprising merchants in 829. Largely Byzantine in its final form, it also displays Romanesque arches, Gothic ornament in the arcades, and four gilded bronze horses of Greek origin, seen in detail on the next page following. The horses, relics of the age of Alexander the Great, were removed from Constantinople at the time of the Fourth Crusade.

Like St. Mark's, the Doge's Palace combines many styles: the inner façade shown on the third plate and again to the right of the fourth has elements of Gothic and Renaissance; the upper tier of the Clock, at the far left of the fourth plate, is Baroque. The Giants' Staircase, near the center of that photograph, was named for the Greek gods Mars and Neptune, who stood at the top. It was on this spot that a newly elected doge received his hat in the traditional Venetian ceremony.

A relic of bygone magnificence, the palazzo on the Grand Canal, shown on the fifth plate, now has a shop on the ground floor which sells blown glass and mosaic. Its façade, once relatively chaste, is decorated today with an overlay of gold mosaic that glitters brightly in the Venetian sun. But the winged lion in the photograph facing it, symbol of Saint Mark, stands as proudly as ever atop one of the famous twin columns on the Piazzetta. And the Church of Santa Maria della Salute, seen in the last picture from the Grand Canal, rises grandly to the blue skies, still an imposing monument to Venice in the hour of her glory.

gaudiness, with the gold and scarlet trappings of the ceremonial barges, and the striped awnings of the palace windows, the deep-red carpets on the landing stages, the flowers and the flags and the bright cotton dresses.

All is heightened and intensified by the curious quality of the light—so capricious or whimsical that sometimes every roof top is etched in a distinct and separate clarity, but sometimes awareness of distance and proportion vanishes, the city loses its sense of depth, and the great façades seem to be no more than backdrops in a toy theatre, as thin and insubstantial as cardboard. *Trompe-l'oeil* is the very essence of Venice, which takes delight not only in confusing your emotions but also in deceiving your senses. Foreshortenings, delusions, quaint deceits, and hallucinations provide half the piquancy of this place, and leave you always rubbing your eyes or consulting your guidebook, wondering if it really is velvet you are seeing, or only a marble imitation; whether that arm really is protruding from the canvas; whether those bells really are swinging out of the ceiling; whether you can in fact walk down that apparent corridor before you, or will only bump your head against a block of masonry. You can never be sure in Venice. She has always been an agnostic city, and has epitomized her doubts in these demonstrations of the fact that seeing is not always believing.

Her texture, too, draws us sensually to her side. She is encrusted with marvelous materials, luxurious of substance and evocative of name—jasper and *marmo greco,* porphyry and cipolin, verd antique, alabaster, granite polished smooth as butter. She is hung about with seductive textiles, such as Wagner used to enrich his apartments on the Grand Canal—the silks, taffetas, velvets, damasks, and satins that helped once to make her rich, in the days when all the delights of the Orient passed this way, fragrant with spices and attended by small apes. Sometimes, when the greasy winter rain falls on Venice, the marbles of the Basilica seem transformed into some glorious brocade. Sometimes even the canals, their waters dimly reflecting flags and old palaces, seem to be covered in shot silk. There

---

A New Skira Book Presents Old Venice

The priceless legacy of the doges is the subject of a new volume, *Treasures of Venice,* created for Horizon by the Swiss art publisher Albert Skira. It contains eighty-five color plates and many black-and-white photographs that range over the great buildings, paintings, sculpture, and other art objects of the city, including the missal which appears on the cover of this issue. The principal text is by the Italian art expert Michelangelo Muraro, former curator of the Doge's Palace and now curator of historic Florentine monuments; while the outstanding authority on Byzantine art André Grabar, of the Collège de France, has contributed a chapter on St. Mark's and its treasures.

---

are moments when the very flagstones of Venice seem to yield beneath your feet, as though you are walking upon some bottomless carpet; and almost any sunny morning, if you sail into the lagoon out of the Adriatic, the tall towers and cluttered palaces of Venice look not so much insubstantial, or even theatrical, but nothing less than edible.

For there is nothing steely about her, nothing even static. People think of her as stagnant, and associate her, as did Thomas Mann, more with Death than with Life. She is, nonetheless, a place of constant dappled movement, easy, gentle, slithery. For every harsh gesture of the irritated tourist, there are a thousand tremulous water shadows on the undersides of bridges. For every angry churning of the *vaporetto* screw, a dozen swift, silent rowing craft spring lithely out of the back canals. Everywhere the gondolas steal secretively by, and the nuns pass noiselessly beneath the arcades, and the old beggar-women sit with a graceful spreading of coarse skirts on the steps of the bridges, and the big ships move grandly through the lagoon, bringing oil from Arabia or sightseers from Manhattan. The policemen in their cocked hats, their faces blessed with an infinite calm vacuity, pace across the Piazza slowly, majestically, rhythmically. The waiters at Florian's, hastening among the outdoor tables, adroitly juggle their little trays. The photographer in the middle of the great square bends over his camera, throwing his black cloth over his head like a hood, as though performing the first prostration in some arcane ritual. Nothing jars, nothing rasps, and life proceeds like some well-greased mechanism of the steam age, brassy but exact.

And in the end, you may decide, the answer to the riddle, the theme of that siren song, is only the very fact of Venice herself—so strange but exciting an organism, her history so magnificent, her setting so melancholy, her people so striking, her continued existence, in a world of gathering conformity, so triumphant an anachronism. You may hate her or distrust her, but like those multitudes of writers and painters, you can never quite forget her. No city inspires in its visitors a more urgent instinct for possession; and conversely no city more generously grants you the feeling that once you have set eyes on her, in a way she is yours. There is a slot in every man's mind for Venice. There, when once she has entered it, she will lie forever, an ever-present evocation of palaces and silent ships, the half-heard cry of a sea bird when you take the train to the office, the distant smell of mud, fish, and old stone as you eat your package lunch, and always the enigmatic temptation of her presence to snatch you away from your noisy chores and urge you home to the lagoon. "There go the swallows to Venice, the stout sea-farers! Seeing those birds fly makes one wish for wings!"

Thus you will feel, too, if you stand before that water color once again, faded above the spare-room mantelpiece, and imagine those ineffable Dawns with Dear Henry long ago, in the spring of 1887.

This is the third in a group of essays on famous cities by Mr. Morris, essayist and correspondent of the Manchester Guardian.

By HERBERT KUBLY

THE CARE AND FEEDING OF ARTISTS

Washington is just now coming to grips with the problem, somewhat nervously,

One sultry summer's afternoon thirty ladies tumbled out of a bus in southern New Hampshire and started over the trails of MacDowell Colony to stalk the artist in his lair. On a tree they saw a sign, "Wild Life Refuge." It started them laughing, and a writer stepped to the door of his studio to investigate the clatter.

"Look!" cried a lady. "There's one!" The writer fled, leaving the woods deserted and quiet and, for the visitors, utterly frustrating.

They could hardly have been aware of the very intense activity all around beneath the quiet surface. In twenty-seven secluded studios, invisible as burrowing animals, writers were working on novels and plays, composers were scoring symphonies, artists were painting. The hidden industry going on since 1908 has made these New Hampshire woods the most creatively prolific rural four hundred acres in America.

The MacDowell Colony is a practical application of an old and recurrent idea. A London editorialist, signing himself "Musophilus" in the *Historical and Literary Register* for July 5, 1745, suggested that Parliament build a hospice for writers on the banks of the Thames; protocol would assign cellar apartments to abridgers and anthologizers and top-floor apartments to ode writers. In J. M. Barrie's *A Window in Thrums* the rustic philosopher Tammas Haggart, lamenting the fate of Robbie Burns, insists that "ondootedly something should be done for geniuses, them bein' aboot the only class as we do naething for." Haggart had in mind a home that would provide "a bit o' garden, whaur the geniuses could walk aboot arm-in-arm composin' their minds." The guests would be sent to bed early because "geniuses' healths is always breakin' doon because of late hours," and a special part of the home would be partitioned off for female geniuses

Except to the downright hungry or to frivolous amateurs, the principal attraction of an artists' colony is neither the bed and board (usually austere) nor the promise of camaraderie (chancy at best); it is what the novelist Catherine Lindsay (The Country of the Young) has found here in a studio at the MacDowell Colony: time to reflect and a place to work undisturbed.

because male geniuses "is no to be trusted wi' womenfolk."

How a society might succor its artists is a question to which President Kennedy is seeking an answer (see "The Kennedy Look in the Arts," HORIZON, September, 1961). His promise of "a New Frontier for American art" has fired the hopes of many, but none of the plans has included anything as elemental as care and feeding. Speaking on a television panel, Russell Lynes, Managing Editor of *Harper's Magazine,* objected to government assistance for artists, which he called "art by committee" and "subsidy for creeping mediocrity." Historical evidence supports him: Tacitus became a propagandist of the Roman state, and the Renaissance poet Lodovico Ariosto celebrated the virtues of his patron duchess, Lucrezia Borgia. To avoid becoming an apologist for his government, Plato fled to Sicily where he hoped to found his Republic.

What, then, of the privately endowed asylum; in other words, the MacDowell idea? (The "idea" also includes America's two other colonies: Yaddo at Saratoga, New York, and the Huntington Hartford Foundation at Pacific Palisades, California, both of which are modeled on MacDowell.)

The retreat in the New Hampshire hills is a widow's memorial to Edward MacDowell, the first serious American composer to win world fame. Born in 1861, MacDowell in his youth was one of life's charmed princelings. His prosperous father sent the strikingly gifted boy to Europe where he caught the fancy of old Franz Liszt, who promoted performances of his work. Known as "the handsome American"—he had ruddy skin, black hair, a red mustache, and the temperament of a thoroughbred—MacDowell was at twenty a popular virtuoso and a famous teacher in the Darmstadt Conservatory. One of his pupils, a pretty, obstreperous American three years his senior, named Marian Nevins, rebelled. "I didn't come all the way to Germany to study with an American younger than myself," she argued. She soon had a change of mind and heart. Recognizing that her own talent would never match his, the the pupil married the teacher and dedicated herself to the advancement of his career. They returned to America where his success both as a composer and a pianist was the greatest any native had yet achieved.

When he was thirty-five, MacDowell, overruling his wife's objections, became the first music professor of Columbia University. It was a time when European training was considered obligatory for American artists. MacDowell had a plan to end this inferiority-complex snobbery by building a vast university arts center to train American artists at home. He was an erratic teacher, dedicated to gifted pupils like John Erskine and Upton Sinclair, and indifferent to the mediocre majority. "Like a dog on his hind legs," wrote MacDowell of his teaching, "I do it, but not gracefully." His situation grew increasingly irksome when the aggressive Nicholas Murray Butler became Columbia's president. The conflict between the two unpliable egoists broke MacDowell's spirit, and in 1904 he resigned.

Marian MacDowell took him to an abandoned sixty-acre farm near Peterborough, New Hampshire, that she had bought in 1896 "for a penny and a mortgage" (actually $1,500). In the forest she built a secluded log studio with a view of Mount Monadnock that MacDowell described as:

> *A house of dreams untold,*
> *It looks out over the whispering treetops,*
> *And faces the setting sun.*

The words were ominously prophetic. For MacDowell the time was already too late. Brooding over the Columbia de-

but for fifty years New Hampshire's MacDowell Colony has known the secret

There are twenty-six studios
at MacDowell, all secluded in the
woods (above) but no two alike.
Composers get pianos, painters get big
north windows. Writers, such as
the satirist John Sack (right), need
only a place for the typewriter.
The author of Report from Practically
Nowhere, *he has written from
time to time for* The New Yorker.

bacle had affected his mind, which now returned to its child-hood. MacDowell spent the last years of his life playing with toys, and died, senile and helpless, at the age of forty-six. The arts center of which he dreamed was finally authorized by Columbia University in 1961, on the centennial of his birth.

In the dark days of her anguish Marian MacDowell thought much of the plight of the artist in a land where materialist expansion was the *kinesis,* a nation of doers in whom contempt for the dreamer was ingrained. She made plans to extend MacDowell's cabin in the woods into a serene workshop where artists could be liberated from the cares of daily life. She had a nest egg of $30,000 that the Mendels-sohn Glee Club of New York had originally raised for Mac-Dowell's care. To augment this she took to the road, giving recitals and lectures. "I didn't play very well, but I did make a lot of noise," she said. Her electrifyingly visionary person-ality charmed money from philanthropists, women's clubs, and music sororities. When she thought she had enough, she went home to buy more land and build studios. She was, as she said, "on fire with a campaign to free the human spirit."

She collected a mighty Parnassus—the names are on the "tombstones," the pine-slab rosters of each studio's occu-pants: Willa Cather, Elinor Wylie, William Rose and Stephen Vincent Benét, DuBose Heyward, Padraic and Mary Colum, Hervey Allen, Aaron Copland, Roy Harris, Douglas Moore, Thornton Wilder, Sara Teasdale, Maxwell Bodenheim, Alfred Kreymborg.

Mrs. MacDowell fussed over her artists as if they were children, nursing their illnesses, dressing their poison-ivy blisters; she delivered their firewood and basket lunches in a two-wheeled buggy hitched to a skittish horse named "Ca-boolian"; and when a sightseer asked her, "Are you one of the help?" she replied, "Yes, I work here." She also ruled her little duchy of the muses like a matriarchal dowager. Liquor was frowned upon; Mrs. MacDowell considered the intoxica-tion of art quite sufficient. Sex was a vulgar preoccupation of the Philistine bourgeoisie, far removed from the innocent joys of creation. To aid her artists toward purity, Mrs. MacDowell banned husbands and wives from the premises, and no one was permitted to enter his unelectrified studio after six P.M. An early and celibate bedtime—after a carefree evening of croquet or poetry—was considered essential for healthful activity. There was rebellion, of course, which Mrs. Mac-Dowell handled with gracious, if forceful, restraint. When rumors reached her that a young poetess was forsaking her own studio for a married novelist's, she called on the liber-tarians and demanded emotionally: "Tell me! Is it a *great* love?" The poetess departed the next day. Some of the sur-reptitious romancing led to marriage, as in the cases of Du-Bose and Dorothy Heyward and William Rose Benét and Elinor Wylie.

More and more, the Colony became a summer gathering of old friends who would get together evenings in Hillcrest, the house where Mrs. MacDowell lived, to play anagrams. When Mrs. MacDowell walked into the room, one or another of several aging vestals would huskily croak, "The Queen! God bless her!" and a reverential cook sometimes recited her own panegyrics in the dining room, beginning, "She is the lily of the valley, she is the song of the lark. . . ."

In spite, or because, of the manacling restraints, the idea was working—and gloriously. In one summer *Porgy, The Bridge of San Luis Rey,* and Edwin Arlington Robinson's *Tristram* were being written in neighboring studios. In the

Four painters lunch together in the "Alexander Studio" (left) at MacDowell. From the left they are Ralph Mayer, his wife Bena Frank Mayer, Gregorio Prestopino, and Elizabeth Dauber Prestopino. The lunch was left outside the door in baskets (below). Mr. and Mrs. Prestopino are former colonists who now have a small summer cabin of their own not far away.

two decades between the wars Mrs. MacDowell's band collected thirteen Pulitzer Prizes. Robinson, nearly always in straitened circumstances, came twenty-four summers and wrote three Pulitzer Prize books.

It came to a climax, this Golden Age, in a disaster. Financially the Colony had seldom risen above a Carthusian austerity, and Mrs. MacDowell was frequently in debt. In 1938 the great New England hurricane swept over the Colony, turning it into an uprooted wasteland. The noble dream, everyone assumed, had ended in a nightmare.

Everyone, that is, but Mrs. MacDowell, eighty-one years old. Like an old circuit rider she returned to the road. On trains between concerts she wrote begging letters. The money was somehow gathered in. Stump pullers and carpenters peopled the Colony in 1939; in 1940 the painters and composers and writers were back.

The storm's scars had still not healed in 1947 when I arrived for the first time. The path of the winds was a swath of new growth. Trillium and lady's-slippers grew in the pits of unmoored pines, and fiddleback ferns stood man-high like vestiges from a coal age.

The Colony was in transition in other ways. Some of the great old-timers were still there. Carl Carmer was a fatherly dean to the young. The painter Elizabeth Sparhawk-Jones, in a black Inverness cape, was like a dark angel hovering over the heath. Molly Colum, aging and raging, a beautiful red-haired Iseult still, thumped her forest stick angrily at a young poet just returned from mass, thundering, "They tell me, young fellow, you're a papist!" Alfred Kreymborg, gentle lutist of words, was virtuoso of the chessboard and pool table as well.

There was also a new generation of youngsters, unproven, promising, filled with hope. In my studio in a thicket of azaleas and jack-in-the-pulpits I was writing a play. In the next studio Lukas Foss (who Mrs. MacDowell hoped would return to music the romance she said was lost with the First World War) was shouting his new oratorio, and at the end of the trail Irving Fine was composing beautifully classic piano pieces. On the hill Esther Geller, the wife of composer Harold Shapero, was cooking wax for the encaustics she was painting that summer. We worked with frenzy—even one wasted moment of such perfection filled us with guilt. Nothing much came of my work those months; nothing, that is, except the most important thing of all, an identity with artists and a confidence for writing. I had been a journalist—that summer I became a writer.

We were a noisy band. Evenings we played four-handed Mozart and Schubert and went to square dances. We told an arriving poet that new colonists were expected, as a courtesy, to enlist in the Peterborough Volunteer Fire Department, and we invented a mythical musicologist, an eminent Dr. Emory Taylor of "Chutney Academy, Chutney Mills, Ohio," whose arrival and departure were reported in detail in the local newspaper. It was a magic summer—I doubt that any of us ever had another quite like it. Some old colonists called us "charging young bulls," and there was talk of expelling us. When this happened, Molly Colum, the one we feared most, chided, "Nonsense! This is no hen yard to be frightened by the shadows of hawks."

Word of our antics got to Hillcrest, and one day Mrs. MacDowell came to see me, driven to my studio by a caretaker. She was a wispy pert bird of a woman wearing a purple dress and hat, white lisle stockings, and black-buttoned shoes. She was nearly blind with cataracts, and she hobbled

At the end of his stay, the Oklahoma composer T. J. Anderson observes a MacDowell tradition by inscribing (above) his name and occupation on the pine "tombstone" that hangs in every studio. Mark Harris (right), whose books include Bang the Drum Slowly *and* Wake Up, Stupid, *gazes out on a vista that is far removed from the gritty urban milieu of his baseball novels.*

on crutches from a hip injury that invalided her the last two decades of her life. She was, she said, delighted to find me working. "In the old days I once visited eleven studios and not one artist was in," she said. And then, as if to let me know that she also had mellowed with the years, she added, "I was dreadfully Victorian. I expected them all to be working." To allay my uneasiness that she might be snooping, she said, "Now I know better. Even if they're not working, I'm sure they're replenishing the spirit just by being here."

She was feeling especially jolly, she said, because of news about a $50,000 legacy that had been held in trust "for two very old ladies in their seventies to live from the income." The word that morning was that "the poor old dears have died. I can't pretend to be unhappy about it." Uncannily perceiving my thoughts, she threw back the broad brim of her hat and coquettishly said, "You really should tell me I don't look ninety. I don't, you know."

I was invited to Hillcrest. In a dark Victorian parlor, facing a bronze bust of her dashing young husband, the old lady reminisced: "In MacDowell I saw what can happen to an artist in America. I don't believe it, the Mozart myth that talent flourishes in adversity. There are after all not many Mozarts, and who can say what he would have accomplished if he'd had a happier life." She was afraid the best poem might be the one that just escaped being written. "It's what I've dedicated my life to prevent—the non-writing of the great poem," she said. "The Colony is my child. I can remember every single one of you who has been here. You young ones, you who were born after the Colony, you are my investment in the future. People keep expecting me to die. I fool them. You see I intend to stay as long as I can to see the returns of my investment."

In my case she just barely did. It was another eight years before I was able to repay her. Mrs. MacDowell died in 1956, just before her ninety-ninth birthday and seven months after my first book won a National Book Award.

If the Colony seemed an amiable place that first year, it was even more genial when I returned nine years later. For the first time in its history it was under male administration, and this was an improvement. The director, George Kendall, had perfected the techniques for pleasing artists, at the same time remaining as remote as possible from their personal lives. This, Mrs. MacDowell and the ladies who succeeded her were never able to do, uninvolvement being essentially a masculine quality. Today the spirit is one of relaxed permissiveness, as befits mature adults. The studios have electricity and running water, and one is free to go there any of the twenty-four hours. There are only two very necessary prohibitions—no uninvited studio visiting before four o'clock and no smoking in the highly inflammable forests. The cocktail hour is a ritual—sometimes in the high summer season there are two or three parties a day. Formerly a summer colony, it is now open all year. Romances—once referred to as "summer lightning"—are frequent, and marriages resulting from them are successful, being based on a mutuality of interests. For practical reasons, since idle individuals are invariably a disturbing influence, uncreative husbands and wives are still not welcomed, but for them there are rooms and apartments available in the village.

The phrase "artists' colony," not surprisingly, conjures up some curious notions. A Chicago businessman wrote to his composer son, "I hope that school will do you some good," and a banker's wife, who has lived all her life within thirty miles of Peterborough, asked at a cocktail party, "Do you

MacDowell's Pulitzers

MacDowell colonists have won twenty-three Pulitzer Prizes for work that, in most cases, was done wholly or in part at the Colony. They are: Margaret Widdemer for poetry in 1919; Edwin Arlington Robinson (top left) for poetry in 1922, 1925, and 1928; Willa Cather (middle left) for *One of Ours* in 1923; Leonora Speyer for poetry in 1927; Stephen Vincent Benét for *John Brown's Body* in 1929 and (posthumously) *Western Star* in 1944; Thornton Wilder (bottom left) for *The Bridge of San Luis Rey* in 1928, *Our Town* in 1938, and *The Skin of Our Teeth* in 1943; Julia Peterkin for *Scarlet Sister Mary* in 1929; Marya Zaturenska for poetry in 1938; John Gould Fletcher for poetry in 1939; William Rose Benét for poetry in 1942; Aaron Copland (top right) for *Appalachian Spring* in 1945; Peter Viereck for poetry in 1949; Douglas Moore for his opera *Giants in the Earth* in 1951; Gail Kubik for his Symphony Concertante in 1952; Ernst Toch for his Third Symphony in 1956; Norman Dello Joio (middle right) for *Meditations on Ecclesiastes* in 1957; Stanley Kunitz for poetry in 1959; and John LaMontaine (bottom right) for his piano concerto in 1959.

have adolescents and is there a department for senior citizens? Do you give public performances of your works on skiing weekends?"

You begin by explaining what a colony is emphatically not. It is no school, no rest home for the frail and self-indulgent, no summer resort for dilettantes, no rompish experiment in aesthetics, no rural outpost of Greenwich Village with Bohemian *déjeuners* under the trees. Simply stated, it is an earnest workshop where working conditions are as nearly perfect as possible. To an outsider MacDowell's most conspicuous characteristic is its churchlike silence. Hidden from one another in the wooded hollows are the studios—small solid cottages equipped with pianos for composers, north windows and easels for painters, typewriters and tables for writers. Each has an open fireplace with plenty of fuel and, in winter, automatic oil heat. At midday a basket lunch is delivered to the door by a silent courier. Artists live in central residence halls near a well-stocked library building and a community house where they meet for breakfast and dinner and for evening games and music. Every artist's caprice is somehow satisfied. When a painter complained that the forest green was dominating his palette, workmen were sent to cut down the offending trees outside his window.

Sometimes there is even inspiration. Thornton Wilder, wandering through the Peterborough streets at twilight, plotted *Our Town* about "Grovers' Corners, New Hampshire," and Aaron Copland, composer of *A Lincoln Portrait* and *Appalachian Spring,* said: "If people find some reflection of the American spirit in my music, then MacDowell must take some of the credit, for it was here that I first experienced the New England I had read about in Brooklyn where I was born." September before last, Louise Bogan's fancy

was dazzled by insects shimmering like air-borne jewels, and she wrote a poem, "The Dragonfly."

For city-bred artists the forest living itself casts a spell. Thrushes, normally twilight singers, are roused to earlier epiphanies by the sounds coming from composers' studios. In winter every studio is a bird commissary. The composer Louise Talma kept a chipmunk named "Igor," and a writer was nearly driven witless by some squirrels that seemed to be operating a bowling alley with hickory nuts in his attic. My pet was a gourmet woodchuck who each morning turned biped and daintily nipped the fresh daisies that had bloomed around my studio during the night. Sometimes the silence can be shattering, as in the case of a painter from New York's Eighth Avenue who requested that a tractor be driven by his studio for one day until he could accustom himself to the quiet.

There are those who question the premise of a colony, who doubt that artists can or should live together at all. I know artists who would prefer colonies of germs or insects to colonies of other artists, and for themselves they are undoubtedly right. Robert Frost is one of these. Another, J. D. Salinger, says, "A writer's worst enemy is another writer." A New York agent warns his clients against "the destructive hazards of living with other artists."

The hazards are certainly real. Paranoia in varying degrees is the occupational disease of art, and the fact must be faced that the constantly bruised sensibilities of artists do not make it easy for them to get along. This is especially true of the unsuccessful amateur, the unrooted would-be talent that sometimes floats through colonies. The worst place to conceal a lack of talent is a colony; the presence of working artists simply magnifies the insecurities and frustrations. As

Marian MacDowell's fierce (and, at the time, visionary) "campaign to free the human spirit" was launched from Hillcrest, the New Hampshire house to which she took her ailing husband. It became the nucleus of the colony. A bust of Edward MacDowell (right) stands enshrined in the parlor, but today it is her indomitable spirit, not his, that permeates this memorial to him.

in any tightly knit group, there will be jealousy; and gossip, a favorite entertainment, can become destructive and ugly. Nearly every summer brings one or two displaced souls seeking a gregarious *vie bohème* who, faced with the reality of long days of solitude, are almost unhinged by it.

Sometimes the anxieties find absurd outlets, as the season when amateur table tippers tried to recall the ghost of Elinor Wylie, or the disquieting summer that a writer professing to be a witch gave instructions in exorcism. One novelist compares colony life to the Army, since he finds it has the same problems and tensions. Perhaps it is more like a ship with many highly charged individuals gathered in an artificial intimacy. The chemistry is compounded several times a year in New York by a conscientious admissions committee that has no way of knowing how the human ingredients will react on one another. "As in all things human, the formula is never constant," says Director Kendall. "Much of the time the blend is smooth and pleasant. It can also happen that it may erupt." An eruption occurred summer before last when a poetess, alarmed by the ebullience of some youthful composers, cried, "Savages! They're all savages!" and lamented that the Colony, as Shaw lamented of youth, was wasted on the young. Remembering the "charging young bulls" of 1947, I held my aging peace.

The individual's success or failure in a colony has less to do with the colony than it has with his relationship to his work. The one thing a colony is not is a garden of muses. There is no magic spring bubbling ideas. Nor is a colony a womb in which to hide from life. An artist, in our frenetic times perhaps more than ever, needs to live in the world to interpret it properly; he will find more stimulation in his daily life in New York or in Pittsburgh than in the quiet woods. But he needs also a refuge from the tensions of the world, an opportunity, as Robert Frost says, for "getting a meaning into a lot of material." The secret is to arrive in a colony possessed by an idea, in other words "married" to a project. Then the tranquil studio and the long undistracted hours work their miracle, and creation flows like a river. A painter, Tony Damato, called it "disciplined liberty," and said, "For the first time in my life I am an absolutely free person and the reason I feel so free is because I am forced into discipline." Novelist Kay Boyle says, "Space opens within and without. I do more writing here in a month than in three months at home."

If Mrs. MacDowell's operation was not perfect, nevertheless her idea is the best yet for aiding artists. Her colony was closely studied by the founders of both Yaddo and the Huntington Hartford Foundation. Perhaps that is why Yaddo seems like an echo from the past, being what MacDowell was in its early years: a closely knit, tightly supervised matriarchy. A majority of Yaddo's guests, invited by the director, Mrs. Elizabeth Ames, are old friends or compliant young admirers. The amosphere is schoolish, with residents kept nervously apprehensive by a flow of notes from the office reminding them, "Your radio was heard playing before four o'clock," or "Please do not use so much water. We have a very small plumbing." A novelist made this comparison: "MacDowell exists for the artist, whereas at Yaddo I am made to feel I exist for Yaddo." A young poet, returning to MacDowell after an interim at Yaddo, said, "It's like coming home after a visit with a rich and difficult maiden aunt."

Both Yaddo and the Huntington Hartford Foundation are richly endowed, and free to the artist. MacDowell, financed by Mrs. MacDowell in the deflated thirties, today

Social life at MacDowell is deferred until four o'clock. It may be a cocktail party, informal music-making, or sitting and talking in a studio (left), but it is relaxed and casual. Work, though, is solitary and intense—whether one confronts it in the studio, like the painter Paul Burlin (below), or under the trees, like the poet Carolyn Stoloff (opposite).

operates on a deficit, and the artist is asked to pay twenty-five dollars a week toward the one hundred twenty it costs—at current prices—to keep him. Unfortunately, the magnetic personality of Marian MacDowell is no longer present to harvest donations. If it is to survive, the Colony will need to find new funds. A foundation director who was asked to help replied, "What is the value in keeping a financial invalid afloat?" He argued that Mrs. MacDowell's Golden Age of talent had never returned.

If it hasn't, the reason lies in the times. The twenties and thirties were innocent decades when artists were still dedicated to pursuing perfection unpressed by time or the unknown fears. Robinson and Cather wrote with fire and love, working two or three years to perfect a book. They cherished the solitude necessary to their art, and they believed in creation as the divinest of joys.

Now it is different. Life has become, for the artist as for all men, urgent and anxious. In literature, dedication to belles-lettres is rare. One need only page through a book-review supplement to see that the emphasis is not on written but packaged books. The successful writer is more apt to employ a stable of researchers in New York than hibernate in a forest hermitage. The problem is the composer's and painter's as well. The composer John La Montaine, the most recent MacDowell Colonist to win a Pulitzer Prize, said, "Can you imagine Schubert thinking of the publicity value of the *Erlkönig*? Or writing it, for example, in response to the demand for songs about death, so that he can get ahead as a composer?"

We can't. Yet these are conditions with which the artist must work today. If the quality of talent seems lower, it may be that the talent no longer has time to develop. No doubt

there are composers and writers too busy for colonies. For those who are not too busy, the colonies in these lean years are serving a more urgent need than ever. If one keeps in mind that less than 2 per cent of all American philanthropy in 1960 went to the arts—including literature—the signs are irrefutable. The death of MacDowell Colony would be a most tragic symbol of a rich nation's disregard for its soul's life.

If the colony has some of the idyllic aspects of a welfare utopia, it is nonetheless based on principles absolutely opposed to the social state. The New Hampshire light is northern, the landscape Chekhovian. Sometimes sitting at the wide window of my studio I gaze over a green meadow at the darkly spired fir forest beyond, or in the winter at a clump of snow-marooned birch, and I imagine I am in a Russian *dacha*, one of the state-owned communities for artists such as the one in which Pasternak lived and died. Looking beyond the light and the scenery, I think of a Russian poet, how both he and I are pampered and coddled, how we are fed and housed and freed from the time-consuming details of practical living. I come to a difference: I think how my Russian brother's imagination is controlled and how mine is free and its freedom is protected. For his pampered life he must write to please authority. For mine I have only to maintain a certain excellence in my work.

Here, for the moment, I am in harmony with the world, and my life, like my work, comes into focus. It is as Edwin Arlington Robinson said in 1922, "absolutely necessary to be here in order to understand what it means."

Herbert Kubly's first book was An American in Italy. *He has since written* Easter in Sicily *and* Varieties of Love, *as well as a novel,* The Whistling Zone, *to be published next month.*

On Screen: JOHN FRANKENHEIMER

Soon after he discovered that his acting was "terrible—stiff and nervous," John Frankenheimer decided to become a director. He was a twenty-year-old undergraduate at Williams College at the time, and his first directorial chore was Noël Coward's *Design for Living*—a production that by his own admission was "one of the worst-staged plays ever done at Williams. I had about as much right to direct it as entering myself as a jockey in the Kentucky Derby. It was an appalling fiasco—the leading actor tripped over a couch, fell flat on his rear end, and everybody forgot his lines."

Now, twelve years, one hundred and twenty-seven television shows, and five motion pictures later, Frankenheimer, the most adventurous young American movie director, is what Hollywood calls "hot." One producer, Martin Manulis, says he is "the most talented director for his age [33] and weight [170] I know." And as anyone who has been on a Frankenheimer set can testify, he is the most flamboyant movie maker since De Mille, flogging the air with his long arms, snapping his fingers with a crapshooter's abandon, crouching like an animal, often slumping to his knees, ripping up his clothes, peppering his instructions with pithy and, very often, impolite language.

Since he fervently holds that "the very process of doing a show is a comment by the director," he makes his comments with graphic force, using fast cuts, trick angles, close-ups to the pore, camera peeps through grilles and keyholes, sometimes at the risk of upstaging the story. In the television version of Daphne du Maurier's *The Little Photographer* he shot one scene as though through a camera's aperture. For *Sailor on Horseback* he used what he calls "a subjective camera"; for example, in a fight between Lloyd Nolan (as Jack London) and the villain, "each man fought a camera and I cut back and forth." Such startlingly realized moments eventually gave him the pick of performers: for *The Browning Version* he secured the services of Sir John Gielgud; for *Turn of the Screw*, Ingrid Bergman; for Faulkner's *Old Man*, Geraldine Page.

Frankenheimer was the youngest—and among the first—of the "live" television directors to pass into movies, where he took in his confident stride some curiously diverse scripts. He shot a poignant *Young Stranger* with James MacArthur, in twenty-five days. He succeeded in making Burt Lancaster behave like an actor in both *Birdman of Alcatraz* and *The Young Savages,* in which a fatal stabbing was reflected in the victim's sunglasses.

Frankenheimer is a dark, lumbering, proud, profane man, half-Jewish, half-Irish, the gangling gentleman son of a New York stockbroker. During his college years, which he "loathed," he embraced rebellion, reacting peevishly to what he felt was "a reactionary pattern . . . a white-shoe conformity." In the Air Force he was attached to a photographic squadron in Burbank, California, where he directed his first film: a documentary dealing with the manufacture of asphalt. His next movie was about cattle. But he did manage to learn something about cameras and composition.

After the service, Frankenheimer walked into CBS's employment office in Manhattan and insouciantly demanded an assistant director's post. "The girl laughed at me, and the head man said, 'You've got lots of nerve.' " As it happened, nerve was enough. It landed him on "weather shows, news shows, Garry Moore, and all that jazz." But before long he was working with Sidney Lumet on *You Are There,* and subsequently with Martin Manulis on the programs *Climax* and *Playhouse 90.* Manulis "took a wild chance on a kid, let me learn, grow, make mistakes, get confidence in myself." Together they followed television West.

Television veterans of the days when shows came live from Hollywood remember the fabled signs that adorned CBS doors with such notices as "This set absolutely closed to everyone. John Frankenheimer." Red Skelton once revised a sign to read: "This set absolutely open to everyone except John Frankenheimer." Unchastened, the young director still insists on privacy. "I can't work with a crowd. And I'm not making movies for an audience in a studio. When you have visitors, *every*one performs." To allay frazzled nerves on the set, he may eat four meals and down three quarts of milk and a wallop of Scotch in a single working day, and smoke three packs of cigarettes. He also loses weight, and characterized *The Manchurian Candidate* as "a fifteen-pound picture."

Although he is sometimes charged with excessive showiness in his directing style, his cleverness with the camera appears to have been put to organic use in *All Fall Down,* his most impressive film to date, and one of America's three entries for the 1962 Cannes Festival. An early shot of a flophouse proprietor in the Florida Keys was taken through an electric fan to underscore the sweaty tedium of the setting. Eva Marie Saint was photographed through mirrors to dramatize her schizophrenia. And the three-ply, tantalizingly slow dissolves of the love scene evoked a lyrical, timeless moment of beauty, in which he "wanted to convey everybody's fantasy of what sex should be and never is."

In his self-proclaimed "search for a means of expression," Frankenheimer's flashy technique has changed little. With each picture, however, his manners on the set grow noticeably less abandoned. "I no longer feel a need to scream," he confesses, and a rapidly fossilizing Hollywood is the poorer for it.   C. ROBERT JENNINGS

35

On Screen: SHIRLEY ANNE FIELD

"You know," she said, "when Marilyn Monroe died all the papers here were after me because we have the same sort of background, but I was away and they couldn't find me. I'm so glad they couldn't find me."

She had just returned to London from a holiday in Italy, and her skin, normally ivory, had turned honey-colored in the sun. She has deep red hair, gray-green eyes, a perfect nose, and a marvelous chin, which she claims is hard to photograph. In repose Shirley Anne Field is unquestionably what the English used to call "a great beauty." When she is laughing (and she is prone to spells of ungovernable hilarity) or telling a story in any one or more of a dozen accents, which is roughly half the time, she becomes a pretty, vivacious child. She is twenty-four.

Shirley Anne Field was born in London's East End but evacuated to a Lancashire orphanage after her home was blitzed. Both the East End and Lancashire swim cheerfully up to the surface in the rich tones of her speech. At fifteen she took a secretarial course and a job with the London Gas Council. At sixteen she won a beauty contest. Acting lessons, modeling jobs, and bit parts in films, plays, variety shows, and television followed. "I've known poverty and I don't like it. I don't care what anyone says; it's demeaning. Acting was the only way I could think of to free myself. But don't overdo the poverty thing. I had to be an actress, anyway."

The small part of the wistful bathing beauty who falls for Laurence Olivier's failing charms in *The Entertainer* lifted Miss Field right out of the starlet category and into *Saturday Night and Sunday Morning* where, opposite Albert Finney, she movingly portrayed a troubled but tenacious young girl. These qualities shimmer phosphorescently in her own character, for her roles and her personality, she acknowledges, have often merged.

The outstanding quality of her performance in *Saturday Night,* one of personal directness and immediacy, establishes itself in her first scene, when she is picked up by Finney in a pub. By avoiding all the cliché facial expressions—coy glances, drooping eyelids, parted lips, and the rest—Miss Field manages to convey her availability as something rare and wonderful, to be won, and won on her terms as much as Finney's. She meets both the demands of the subtly conceived part and of the self-confident Finney, in his role of a young English factory hand already involved in an affair with a married woman. During this brief scene Miss Field communicates far more than sensuality, including something of the woman behind the actress; and her sustained performance—through to the final scene on a new housing estate outside Nottingham, where she reveals herself as just as strong as Finney all along—sets her apart from other young

actresses. In a sense she is set apart from herself, as though to her Shirley Anne Field were a third person, a more or less temporarily valuable commodity. She is professional; she is serious. She knows she is a beautiful girl who can act. About everything else she is not so sure.

Recently she moved into an apartment in London's Kensington district, an area five miles and a world away from her birthplace. It is the first time she has had an opportunity to "fix up a place" for herself, and she is touchingly eager to show visitors what she is doing—more eager, in fact, than to discuss her latest parts in *The Damned,* a science-fiction thriller about a group of radioactively contaminated children living underground, and *The War Lover,* an adaptation of John Hersey's novel in which she stars with Robert Wagner and Steve McQueen. It is perhaps characteristic of her that among all the things that happened during the making of this undistinguished film, she remembers best the head cold that she and Robert Wagner passed back and forth "about seven times."

Tucking her legs beneath her, gazing through her interviewer and back over her twenty-four years, she wondered aloud what had become of the ambition that drove her all this distance. She jumped up abruptly and trailed around the room, touching a scrapbook and a framed photograph of herself almost as though she thought she'd mislaid her ambition somewhere in the apartment.

Where is Shirley Anne Field now? She doesn't really know. Her character, as well as her career, is in transition. She uses all the old phrases—"I don't want you to quote me on that but . . . I don't know why I'm telling you this but . . . I don't want to sound like a cynic but . . . I'm still just a virgin in show business but . . ."—and in the middle of them she will suddenly throw back her head and laugh delightedly, so that the tired words have a new freshness.

Unlike many actors, Shirley Anne Field reads, and is genuinely interested in all sorts of people, not just herself and other actors. She seems to want to sponge up experience and human beings, and not merely for what use she can make of them. What next? John Mortimer, one of England's leading playwrights, is writing a movie about jazz musicians called *The Gigsters* for her, and she has just finished shooting another Mortimer film, *The Lunch Hour,* in which she plays two parts at once—a businessman's wife and his girl friend. She claims to have been "terribly frightened" about managing two roles. Actresses are always saying they are frightened but one believes Shirley Anne Field, for despite all her friends, her agent, her secretary, her publicity man, her twelve accents, she seems utterly on her own.

ROBERT GUTWILLIG

Photograph by PETER BASCH

AFRICA: THE FACE BEHIND THE MASK

Its primitive an

By BASIL DAVIDSON

vage profile, modern scholars are discovering, has obscured a rich and cultivated history

Whether in the range of history, archaeology, social anthropology, or the arts, we are in the presence of a major shift in attitude toward the depth and scope of humanity's enterprise in Africa. Almost until the other day it was commonly held and argued that the cultures of that continent—as they were represented, for example, by their sculpture—were the product of a more or less timeless and primitive innocence, possessing value chiefly as tributes to spontaneous emotion or as objects of art that were essentially artless. Here in this mask, it was explained, we may see how Adam experienced fear, or there in that one, baffling by its strangeness, how Eve knew joy. This was the dawn and infancy of mankind. Everything here had stayed motionless in primal bliss and horror. In the words of a former governor of Nigeria, voicing a familiar thought: "For countless centuries, while all the pageant of history swept by, the African remained unmoved—in primitive savagery."

Today it is increasingly seen and written that the truth about old Africa was seldom or never like this, and that the number of surviving peoples of whom this could ever have been said is so small as barely to exist. Perhaps it may be true that the Pygmies of the Congo forest or the Bushmen of the Kalahari desert still live in a society that was fashioned during the Stone Age; so that one may reasonably regard them, or some of them, as little different in their daily life from the men who painted and engraved on rocks through all the centuries of a remote past. Even this is doubtful, since the lives of Pygmies and Bushmen have long been influenced—and, especially with the Bushmen, gravely damaged and distorted—by the presence and pressure of other kinds of people. What at all events we may be sure of is that the vast majority of Africa's populations have walked the wending stones of time and social change, lifting themselves from the primitive to the less primitive, in much the same way as everyone else in the world. The scenery and the methods have been greatly different, but not the general course and destination. One by one our old fixations about Africa go quietly to pieces.

Quietly, no doubt. For none of this has been much noticed in the world at large or, where it has been, readily welcomed and accepted. There is nothing very surprising in this reluctance: what other peoples have thought and often still think about Africans must drag along with it a heavy weight of ancient and accustomed prejudice. The stereotype of "savage Africa" was cast in Elizabethan times, if not earlier, and the mold has grown rock-hard since then. In European judgments of African culture there has been remarkably little advance since Father Cavazzi, to pick a random but characteristic example, gave his views on African dancing in the Congo of three hundred years ago. "Having no object in the skillful talent of displaying the movement of the body or the agility of the feet," he decided, "dancing among these barbarians serves only the vicious satisfaction of a libidinous appetite." With the twist and other joyful exercises in our midst, this description of the samba may be thought a little uncharitable, not to say downright absurd; but

the fact is that Cavazzi was offering a true reflection of the profound contempt that white men have usually felt, then and long afterward, for the moral and intellectual content of the black man's culture.

Contempt grew into a conviction, later on, that the real trouble with Africans was that they had failed to "grow up" and were therefore lacking in some ingredient of the capacity to achieve a mastery over environment, which men have generally recognized as civilization. This paternalistic view of Africans as feckless or retarded children was largely minted by the early explorers. Once an African grows beyond his childhood years, declared Sir Richard Burton, "his mental development is arrested, and thenceforth he grows backwards instead of forwards." The colonizer, according to a Belgian veteran of the Union Minière copper-mining concern in Katanga, "must never lose sight of the fact that the Negroes have the spirits of children." To which a Portuguese authority on Angola added that the "raw native" must be looked on as "an adult with a child's mentality." French records are full of similar opinions.

The reasons for thinking otherwise are many and various. Quite apart from any conclusions that may be drawn from the political evidence of modern Africa, the face behind the mask of traditional Africa now seems altogether different from what we thought it was. Its features may still appear strange and hard to interpret, but the words "primitive" and "childish" are clearly out of place in trying to describe them. Already we can trace the outline of an African "pageant of history" in which the protagonists, far from remaining "unmoved in primitive savagery," have manifestly traveled a long way from their starting point. We can find in traditional African thought, however unexpectedly, a prescientific maturity and sophistication

A "Dark" Continent Finds its History

The Africa shown opposite, newly emerging from the distortions of myth and prejudice, possesses a complex and dynamic history, a past rich in diversity and change. More than two thousand years ago, for example, the knowledge of iron smelting began to spread southward and eastward from the Kushite kingdom of Meroë, altering tribal societies as it went. Contrary to what was once believed the Africans, and not the Phoenicians, built the walled stone city at Zimbabwe in what is now Rhodesia. Within Africa itself were generated the creative energies of the spirited Nok culture, and of its skilled artistic descendants in Ife and Benin. From as far away as China, outside influences have always been at work in Africa, especially through the Islamic eastern coast; and when the gold trade across the Sahara began to thrive, in medieval times, it built the prosperity of the cultivated city-states of the Upper Niger. The arrival of the Europeans was in fact only another chapter in a long story.

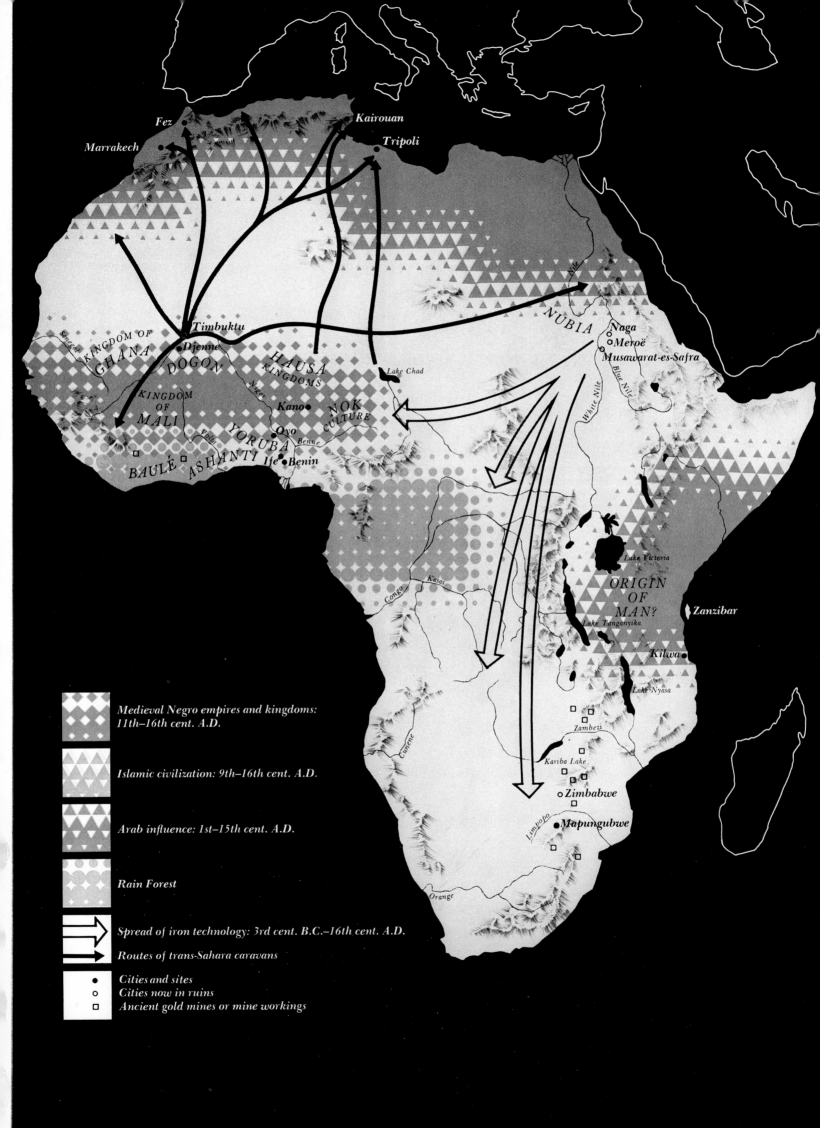

Fez
Kairouan
Marrakech
Tripoli
Timbuktu
KINGDOM OF
GHANA
Djenné
DOGON
NUBIA
Naga
Meroë
Musawarat-es-Safra
HAUSA
KINGDOMS
Lake Chad
Senegal
Niger
KINGDOM OF
MALI
Kano
NOK
CULTURE
Oyo
Benne
White Nile
Blue Nile
Volta
YORUBA
Benue
BAULÉ
ASHANTI
Ife
Benin
Nile
Kasai
Congo
ORIGIN
OF
MAN?
Lake Victoria
Zanzibar
Lake Tanganyika
Kilwa
Lake Nyasa
Zambezi
Kariba Lake
Zimbabwe
Cunene
Limpopo
Mapungubwe
Orange

Medieval Negro empires and kingdoms:
11th–16th cent. A.D.

Islamic civilization: 9th–16th cent. A.D.

Arab influence: 1st–15th cent. A.D.

Rain Forest

Spread of iron technology: 3rd cent. B.C.–16th cent. A.D.

Routes of trans-Sahara caravans

• Cities and sites
○ Cities now in ruins
□ Ancient gold mines or mine workings

Awareness of Negro Africa by the ancient Egyptians appears as early as this wall painting (opposite) from the tomb of Huy, or Amenhotep, viceroy in Nubia during the reign of Tutankhamen (c. 1361–1352 B.C.). In it the Nubian princes are shown doing homage—bringing gold, animal skins, and black giraffe tails (the latter were highly prized) to Tutankhamen, while behind them comes a princess in a chariot drawn by oxen, a parasol of ostrich feathers crowning her diadem. In the Nile plain north of Khartoum the ruins still remain of Nubian cities, like Meroë (above) and Naga (top), but far too little excavating has been done to indicate what manner of civilization flourished here—except that it was a rich and powerful one, trading as far afield as India and China, and profoundly influencing the rest of Africa.

that are emphatic in their projection of dynamic and coherent ideas about man and the universe. We can see in many of the arts of Africa, as a distinguished Italian ethnologist has lately written, the impulse of "ancient and elaborate traditions: not works of exuberant youth and still less of childish inexperience, but products of conscious and thoughtful maturity."

These conclusions rest on a large quantity of obscure and detailed work, much of which has been recorded only in specialist journals whose findings seldom reach a wide public. In the past ten or twenty years anthropologists have ceased to measure African skulls for the purpose of speculating on the relative inferiority of African brains—wisely, since the evidence of man-ape fossils proves in this respect distressingly perverse—and have got down to the task of analyzing how Africans have solved or tried to solve their material and moral problems. Archaeologists have begun to sketch an ordered survey of African ruins and remains, and have dug most usefully at several important sites. Historians have embarked on the systematic collection of African social traditions, relating these where possible to the memoirs of travelers and traders from Europe and elsewhere whose writings—often of outstanding value, if sometimes fabulous and almost always needing fresh interpretation —cover a period of more than a thousand years. And the outcome of all this has been so startling as really to deserve the name of a revolution in thought.

It now appears that the earliest types of men, including our own type, were born in Africa possibly as long ago as two million years. All these experiments in evolution except our own were unsuccessful. None of them got beyond the earliest forms of Stone Age culture. They died out, leaving little but a handful of fossils. Our own type adapted itself and slowly multiplied. There is fairly capacious evidence for this in fossils and fragments, dating back some ten thousand years and more to a period when *Homo sapiens* had long since occupied many other parts of the earth. Modern varieties of *Homo sapiens* in Africa begin to turn up, in more or less easily recognizable fossil form, for the period beginning about seven thousand years ago. In the patient centuries that followed, these peoples began painting and engraving on rocks, notably in the Sahara, which was then a green and fertile land.* They seem to have lived in many regions of northern, central, and southern Africa but were few and far between. Some of them, certainly those who dwelt in the lower valley of the Nile, had established themselves in semipermanent settlements and were growing food by about 4000 B.C. This New Stone Age, signified by the invention of agriculture, moved gradually across the continent.

So far, so good: most of this, after all, is part of a widely accepted prehistory. Then came a radical change. A few centuries before the Christian era Africa south of the Sahara emerged from the New Stone Age into an age of metals, specifically an Iron Age; and it is with new understanding of the course and spread of this Iron Age that fresh perspectives in thought about ancient Africa begin to appear and take control.

*See "Surprise in the Sahara," in HORIZON for May, 1959.

Far from "staying in the Stone Age until the day before yesterday," as the familiar myth would have it, most Africans to the south of the great desert (though the division from North Africa is largely artificial) are now seen to have entered an Iron Age not many centuries after northern Europe. This is the long and complex period, beginning about 200 or 300 B.C., in which most of the traditional societies and cultures of the continent were born.

Techniques of iron smelting and forging induced new kinds of social organization. The technology of iron underlay the early empires of the Western Sudan, shaping the political birth of ancient Ghana, for example, whose central authority seems to have crystallized out of tribal rivalries not long after A.D. 300. Of Ghana an early medieval Arab writer could remark that its warriors made expeditions "with swords and with lances" against neighbors "who know not iron and fight with bars of ebony." But the Iron Age did much more than promote imperial systems in the bare grasslands of West Africa: still more tellingly, it also opened routes of southward migration into the dense forests of Central Africa and the upland plains that lay beyond. Use of the iron-pointed spear and the tighter social cohesion that was linked to it ensured easy conquest over Stone Age peoples already in sparse occupation of those lands, gave better defense against dangerous animals, promoted more successful hunting, and cleared more land for cultivation. By the end of the first millennium A.D., iron-using peoples from west-central Africa had penetrated far across the southern continent. Long before Europe's first large-scale invasion, opening with the settlement of the Cape of Good Hope in 1652, Iron Age peoples whose origin had been far in the north were in strong possession of the central and southern continent almost as far as the Cape itself.

In this way, by wave after wave of migration and settlement through many centuries, inland Africa received the ancestors of most of the peoples who live there today. They advanced in social organization as well as in space. They evolved more complex and efficient forms of government, invented new means of agriculture through irrigation or ingenious tropical farming, developed mining industries wherever valuable ores could be found on or near the surface, split themselves into many communities and nations, and gradually established the traditions of a rich and various culture whose special tone and accent ring out clearly even today. And it is this slow but steady spreading of related peoples that explains both the maturity and the underlying unity of ideas, beliefs, and customs which have controlled men's behavior, and still to some extent control it, throughout much of the continent.

Study of this specifically African culture has lately added or begun to add another new dimension to the picture of Africa's past and present. Here we find, with increasing research, a common stock of philosophical and metaphysical speculation and belief. Not long ago it would have seemed pretentious and perhaps absurd to speak in any such terms of the kind of

"fetish mumbo-jumbo" that pagan Africans were thought to revere. Lately, however, a number of painstaking inquiries into African concepts of God and man and nature have revealed systems of thought that overturn, as the French ethnologist Marcel Griaule pointed out after living with the Dogon of the Western Sudan, "all previous ideas about the mentality of black peoples." Griaule has told how he listened to an old man called Ogotommeli for three and thirty days and found this Dogon sage had laid out for him a conceptual structure about man and the universe that displayed "an internal coherence, a secret wisdom, and an apprehension of realities"—at a prescientific level, needless to say—"equal to that which we Europeans conceive ourselves to have attained."

The general source of these ideas is not hard to trace. It is clear that a way of life which comprehended the major human achievement of peopling huge regions of a hot and difficult continent, and was closely linked to kinship settlement and subsistence farming, produced in time its own characteristic framework of belief. One can see this, to take a single instance, in the so-called "ancestor cult" and its attitudes to land ownership. "I conceive that land belongs to a vast family," commented a Nigerian chief some fifty years ago, "of which many are dead, few are living, and countless members are still unborn." From a number of convictions such as this, jointly held as they are by most communities in Africa south of the Sahara, there has flowed what can reasonably be called a basic unity of culture.

Faced with these unsuspected dimensions of depth of time and breadth of thought, we clearly require a new approach to the arts of Africa. For they in turn will be found to reflect this long-enduring process of migration and settlement over apparently limitless plains and forests that the history of the African Iron Age encompasses. They are the works of an age of faith, an age that was pagan and peculiar to itself, severely limited in many ways, yet all-embracing in its imperatives and finally successful in reaching a notable level of moral and material stability. These masks and figures are not, as someone has penetratingly observed, points of departure but points of arrival. They do not come from the "beginning of time." They occur at the end of a long development.

I should like to illustrate these various points by referring to the famous sculpture of the old Yoruba state of Ife and of its

Trade had already drawn European attention south of the Sahara by the time the Jewish cartographers of Majorca, in 1375, produced the so-called Catalan atlas of Abraham Cresques, from which the map (opposite) is taken. Though the shape of Spain (upper left) can be seen, the geographical information is too sketchy to be useful—including a nonexistent mountain range (center) bisecting the desert. What interests historians is the Negro king at lower right, Musa Mali of Guinea, of whom the text states: "So abundant is the gold which is found in his country that he is the richest and most noble king in all the land."

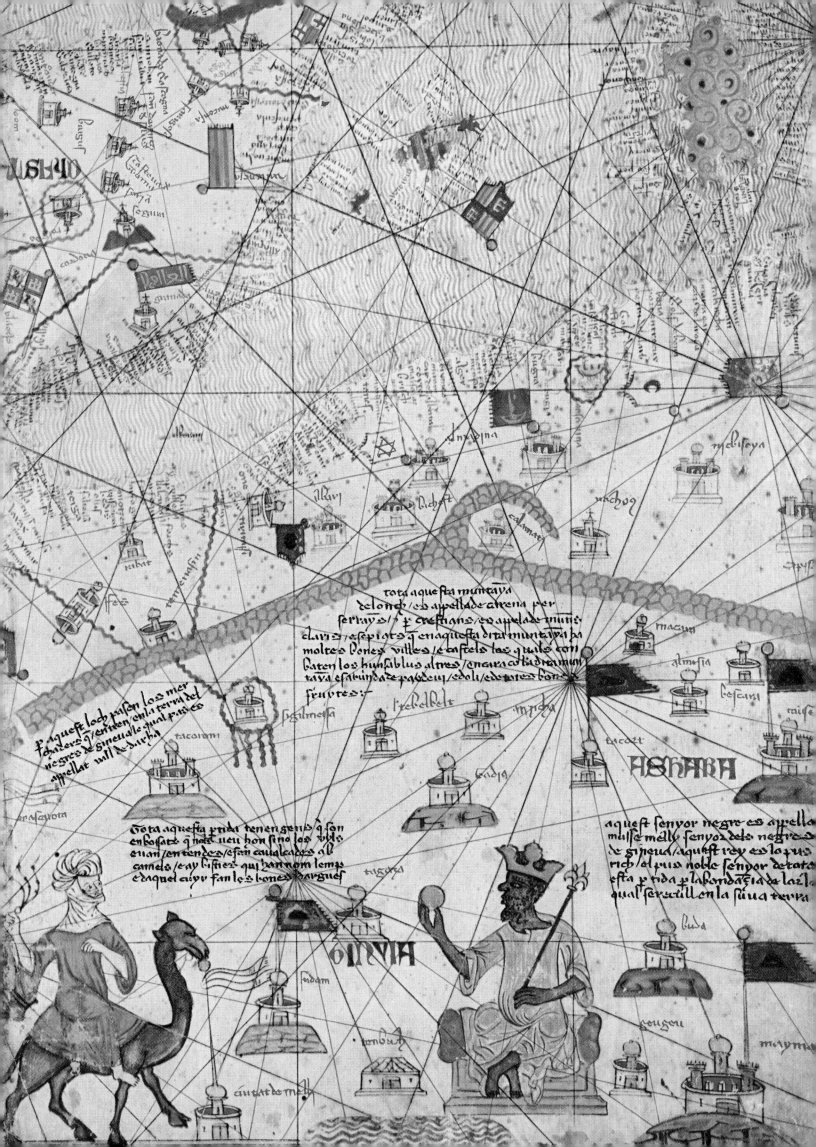

no less well-known successor, Benin. These splendid works have been justly admired, for they are strong and sensitive and beautiful. Yet it is hard to deny that they have owed a good deal of their fame to their anthropomorphic naturalism. Here at last, we have tended to think, is something we can understand—something civilized, classical, or even possibly Renaissance. And so powerfully persuasive has been the myth of the primitive savage that early judgments on this sculpture were unanimous in awarding it a European inspiration. A wandering Italian artist? Perhaps a Greek of ancient times? Or why not a Portuguese? Even today, when it may be shown by historical evidence and latterly by archaeological proof that Ife sculptures are probably older than the Renaissance and certainly much anterior to the arrival of the Portuguese in West Africa, well-intentioned men and women find it difficult to believe these works are truly African.

Nonetheless it is true that the sculpture of Ife and that of Benin stand squarely within the African tradition, being eccentric only to the point that the societies which produced them had developed highly centralized forms of divine kingship and a corresponding requirement from their artists. There is in this respect a most illuminating comparison to be made between the courtly arts of Ife and Benin—ranging from the "pure naturalism" of some of the Ife heads to the hieratic caricatures of decadent Benin—and the wonderfully varied and much more "popular" arts of the peoples over whom the kings and great chiefs ruled. Contrast, for example, a typical chiefly figure of Benin (see page 49) with the superbly stylized leopard now in the Museum of Primitive Art (see page 48). We are obviously in the presence of a most variable and even individual approach; and this impression is repeated and remarkably enlarged by the great diversity of old Nigerian works in metal, such as the Tsoede figures or the group of fine bronzes lately recovered from eastern Nigeria and much else besides, not to mention the parallel achievements of neighboring peoples like the Baulé and Akan.

But let us remain, for the purposes of this essay, with the tradition of Ife and Benin. If completely African, then how and through what diversity of experience did it emerge? Here we enter the realm of speculation, but the speculation begins to be tied persuasively to factual probability and even certainty.

The Yoruba people who built the old empire of Oyo, whose "holy city" was Ife, are now believed to have entered their historical homeland at about the same time that the Normans began casting envious eyes on Anglo-Saxon England. But these newcomers to southern Nigeria were not, if I may quote myself, "the only ancestors of Yoruba civilization, any more than William of Normandy's four thousand knights were the only ancestors of British civilization. They were a relatively small group of travelers, but hard-tried and well-armed: they conquered and settled and were then absorbed among the peoples whom they had found." Yet what kind of people were the "Anglo-Saxons" of southern Nigeria?

TEXT CONTINUED ON PAGE 53

The Acme of African Art

The discovery in northern Nigeria of the two-thousand-year-old Nok culture, of which the head above is a magnificent example, has provided at last a suggestion of whence came, by the thirteenth century, the serene and naturalistic sculptural style of the kingdom of Ife to the south. The terra-cotta head opposite, of a classical simplicity rivaling European efforts at a comparable time, stands at the peak of Ife realism and sophistication. It was disinterred in the latter part of 1957, by ditchdiggers in the environs of Ife who came upon a treasure of four heads in clay and seven in bronze. These were but the latest of numerous discoveries at Ife, which established its preeminence as the Greece of ancient Africa.

DRAEGER—*Connaissance des Arts*; LEFT: BERNARD FAGG—JOS MUSEUM

Together with Ife, the center of African artistic creativity was the kingdom of Benin, sometimes called "bloody Benin," after the persistence of its brutal sacrificial customs and the massacre of a British expedition that took place there in 1897. Benin bronzes, now world-famous for their authority and skill, include the leopard at left, a symbol of the power of Benin's king, or Oba, who often kept tame leopards in his palace. Among the Oba's possessions, when a punitive British expedition came to chastize him, was the ivory mask at right, bearing European heads around its crown and slits in the forehead, eyelids, and eyes to receive inlaid metal: one of the finest works of art we have from Benin, or elsewhere.

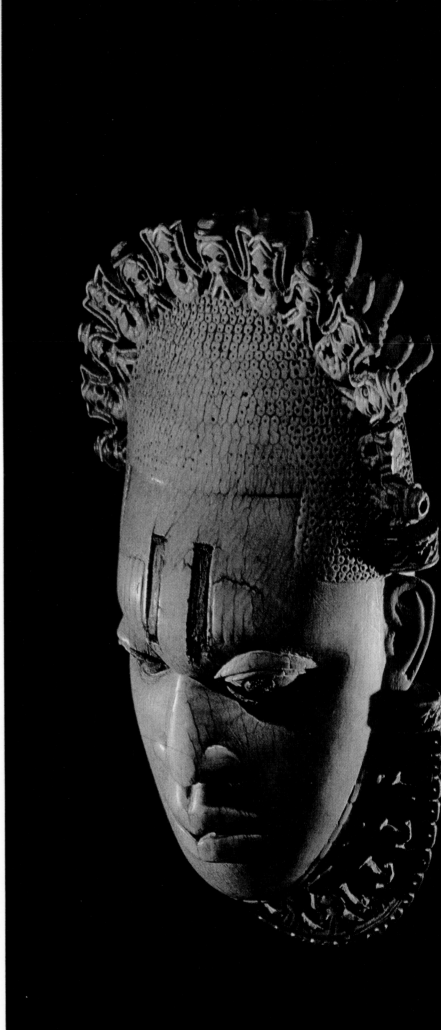

Royal Ease Along the Niger

The walls of the palace of Benin's Oba were decorated with bronze bas-relief plaques, of which approximately eight hundred survive. Usually dated from the late sixteenth to the early eighteenth centuries, these were made by the so-called lost wax process, in which a wax model is surrounded by a clay mold, so that the wax can then be melted out and replaced by molten metal. Most of the plaques, like the powerfully shaped example opposite, were representations of the Oba's majesty and aura, displaying a style in which distortion conveys a sense of his somber authority. The figure at center is of course the Oba, wearing the "choker," or necklace, that is the Bini badge of royalty; the attendants who hold up his hands are presumably minor servants, while more substantial courtiers shield him from the African sun. Bronze casting is still practiced at Benin, though as a cultivated handicraft rather than as a necessity of civic ceremonial.

The most extraordinary work of art ever to come to light in Negro Africa is probably the seated figure (above) first reported in 1921 at Tada, an obscure village on the banks of the Middle Niger. Together with a number of other sculptures, it forms a group known as the Tsoede bronzes, after the semi-legendary Nigerian hero who is said to have been responsible for leaving them in the locations where they were discovered. These figures pose one of the most striking of the many problems confronting the historian of Nigerian art, if only because they include the four largest cast bronzes ever found in Africa, outside the frontiers of Imperial Rome.

It was early in the sixteenth century, according to the traditions of the Nupe and the Igala peoples, that Tsoede, or Edegi, a bastard son of the Ata of Idah, fled up the Niger during a dynastic conflict, taking with him a store of metal heirlooms that included these bronze figures. Before founding the Nupe royal dynasty, he is supposed to have deposited some of them at various stopping places along the river, where they have become sacred insignia of divine kingship. Of these objects, the figures found at Tada, along with two others from twenty-five miles upstream at Jebba, are the most important. It is indeed astonishing to find in a remote riverside village so advanced an example of the spiral in sculptural form, in marked contrast to the rather rigid front view almost universally observed in African art. The posture, in fact, is remarkably close to that known to Orientalists as "royal ease." It could have been made only by a bronze founder of the Ife school, and so may date from the fourteenth century.

WILLIAM FAGG, *Deputy Keeper,*
Department of Ethnography, British Museum

Cattle were much prized by the Egyptians, as they are today by many Africans, especially the tall Watutsi of Ruanda and Burundi, among whom they serve as a feudal form of wealth. What is remarkable is the extent to which African cattle still resemble the "Hathor" cows of Egyptian bas-reliefs, such as the one (above right) from the temple of the Fourth Dynasty King Khuf-wy. The contemporary cow, with the same long curling horn (right) is one of a breed maintained by the Fulani, a nomadic Moslem people who live scattered across the southern edge of the Sahara from Senegal to northern Nigeria. The Fulani are of Middle Eastern rather than Negro racial inheritance, and may originally have migrated from upper Egypt, bringing their livestock with them. They now do a brisk trade in cattle horns, shipping them to Texas to be sold as souvenirs.

TEXT CONTINUED FROM PAGE 46

Nothing useful could be said about this until a few years ago. Today, thanks initially to accidental discoveries by tin miners in central Nigeria, we know a good deal more about the kind of reply that will eventually be made. These "non-Yoruba ancestors" were the highly artistic and ingenious people of the Nok culture, so called after the name of a village where some of their characteristic terra-cotta figures were first recovered. The diligence and devotion of Bernard Fagg, Nigeria's Federal Director of Antiquities, have brought together at the museum in Jos an astonishing display of Nok heads and figures. What is more, a fairly reliable stratigraphy of the region has linked them to a distant period, while radioactivity tests by the Carbon-14 method have yielded boundary dates of 900 B.C. and A.D. 200. We also know that the Nok people had emerged from the Stone Age. They were smelting iron and forging iron tools and weapons.

Here, excitingly enough, were some of the cultural beginnings of Iron Age society in West Africa. But the Nok discoveries have continued. Nok objects are now being found over an increasingly wide area round the confluence of the rivers Niger and Benue, reaching westward into what is Yorubaland today and what was once the territory of the Yoruba empire of Oyo. Can it be that the arts of Ife have at last found their origin? Parallels of style between Nok and Ife, both in form and content, are often strikingly clear (see pages 46 and 47).

To these material indications the legends of the Yoruba add a persuasive gloss. All the various sections of this nation trace their origin to the city of Ife—the "fabled spot," as one of their historians has written, "where God created man, white and black, and from whence they dispersed all over the earth." With this, indeed, we seem to catch the echo of those early migrations which peopled the central and southern lands of Africa. However that may be, the certain fact is that the Yoruba took over a tradition which they found among the populations with whom they settled; and this, evidently, was a Nok tradition.

But then the Yoruba also have another tradition, parallel but contradictory. They believe that they came "from the East," from the lands of the Nile or even beyond; and for this there is some partial confirmation in a number of their cultural traits. "They seem," one expert has concluded, resuming the evidence, "to have come from the east or the northeast, possibly from Meroë." And with that one may well think hard and think again, for the mention of Meroë in this connection has intriguing possibilities.

Meroë (see page 43) was the capital of the Kushite state that flourished on the Middle Nile between the sixth century B.C. and about A.D. 320, when its last ruler was overthrown by the armies of Abyssinian Axum. Little is known of this Kushite state. Its written language is not yet understood. Its monuments have barely felt the prod of the archaeologist's pick and trowel. Its royal tombs, true enough, have yielded king-lists for an unbroken period of nearly one thousand years, but its far-spread "city mounds" have yet to undergo any systematic in-

TEXT CONTINUED ON PAGE 57

Traveling up the Blue Nile in 1772, the Scots nobleman James Bruce was astonished to see parading before him a troop of magnificent cavalry, all wearing chain mail. He could see the same today. A common African tradition holds that these suits of interlocked metal rings (not always in perfect repair) come originally from the Crusaders, and have been handed down from soldier to soldier over the centuries. Probably many are of far more recent, if not actually current, manufacture. The horseman above is one of over three thousand who gathered in northern Nigeria in 1959 to celebrate their newly won independence. OVERLEAF: It is the custom for these riders, many abreast, to come charging up to their ruler, the Sardauna of Sokatu, halting suddenly and saluting him as a pledge of allegiance.

53

The Lure and Allure of Gold

Africans not only traded gold, by way of the caravans across the desert, they worked in it themselves with high artistry. The three gold ornaments at left, two pendant masks and (center) a scorpion ring, testify to the skill of the Baulé, a tribe of the Ivory Coast that migrated there in the eighteenth century, after some dynastic disagreements in the kingdom of Ashanti, taking their metalworking techniques with them. The height of Ashanti achievement in gold is suggested by the two-thirds life-sized mask (above) of King Kofi Kakari, the sole surviving object from what must once have been an extensive royal treasury in a court of lavish pomp and splendor. Ashanti rulers came to greet the early European explorers so heavily adorned in gold that their region was called "the Gold Coast" until the name was changed to "Ghana" in 1957.

TEXT CONTINUED FROM PAGE 53

vestigation. All that may be said with confidence is that Meroë was the lavish capital of an important and relatively advanced African civilization which had borrowed much from Egypt, had felt the impact of ideas along the old trading routes from India and Arabia and even China, and had played in its day and age a crucial part in the southward transference of iron-working technology. Arguing from the presence there of large mounds of slag, a British archaeologist of fifty years ago even thought that Meroë deserved to be called—if with some poetic licence—"the Birmingham of ancient Africa."

Readers of the Acts of the Apostles will have heard of Meroë in another connection. There it is recorded how the Deacon Philip met and baptized a certain Ethiopian dignitary on "the way that goeth down from Jerusalem to Gaza." And "behold, a man of Ethiopia, a eunuch of great authority under Candace, queen of the Ethiopians, who had the charge of all her treasure and had come to Jerusalem for to worship, was returning, and sitting in his chariot read Esaias the prophet." But "Ethiopian" was the old Greek word for Kushite, and the queen mentioned in this passage lived not in Abyssinia but almost certainly amid the pillared comfort of Musawarat-es-Safra, whose imposing ruins may still be seen not twenty miles from Meroë, or seventy miles from Khartoum, lying like noble hulks aground in the waste of the Butana desert.

Now if it is true—and it seems to be—that the intrusive ancestors of Yoruba civilization came from the Middle Nile, perhaps in consequence of the disasters of Axumite invasion in the fourth century A.D., may this not be a comprehensive explanation of the many similarities of religious cult that undoubtedly exist? The sanctity of rams, the supernatural power of snakes, the hierarchy of the Yoruba pantheon: are they not the fragments of a culture brought initially from the Nile? It may be so. Yet at this point of inquiry one should guard against any kind of facile diffusionism that would attribute Negro cultural origins, at least on the religious side, to the ancient cultures of the Nile. It is rather a question, on closer examination, of the chicken and the egg.

For even if it is correct that the "Followers of Horus," semi-legendary founders of dynastic Egypt before 3000 B.C., had entered their kingdom from the Middle East—from *outside* Africa—the fact remains that they found other folk in occupation of the land, and these other folk were undoubtedly African and quite possibly Negro. Where had this "oldest" Egyptian population found its cultural beliefs? The notion that the ancestor-wanderers of the Yoruba first brought to West Africa the idea of snake sanctity, for example, or that of anthropomorphic sculpture, falls down as soon as one considers the Nok figures. For the Nok people, it turns out, already possessed these ideas. Had their forefathers received such ideas from Egypt or had they given them to Egypt? At this stage the right conclusion seems to be that we have come upon the scattered survivals of an ancient cultural interplay between the valley of the Nile and continental Africa, linked to Iron Age beginnings but resting

The legendary land of Ophir, where the gold of King Solomon was mined, seemed to have been discovered in Southern Rhodesia when the first white settlers found the region filled with hundreds of abandoned mine workings and many stone ruins, the greatest of them a high-walled fortress (above) called Zimbabwe. The Europeans preferred not to believe that Zimbabwe, with its massively constructed battlements and towers, could have been the work of Negro Africans, and thus they ascribed it to the remote past, so that it could be credited to wandering Sabaeans or Phoenicians. Unhappily for legend, modern archeologists have been at work on Zimbabwe and have given it a radiocarbon date. For the most part they now agree that the site was occupied from about A.D. 500 to A.D. 1750— and the walls built by native Africans alone.

Ancient and modern in Africa seem often to exist side by side. Hanging beads like those to be seen on the bronze heads of former Obas of Benin (left), symbolizing the tradition that they did not often show themselves to their people, are worn by a present-day ruler (opposite), Oba Ademuwagun Adesida II, Deji of Akure. He is the forty-second Deji to hold this exalted post, and his beadwork costume of stylized leopard faces, weighing over twenty pounds, is a hundred years old. Yet he holds a law degree from Dublin and has been admitted to the London bar. He is an Anglican, but also has ten wives.

on much older African foundations. Here, once again, is the echo of profound unity within the diversity of many cultures.

The same conclusion is likely to emerge from any detailed history of African culture that may be attempted in the future with fuller knowledge: an interweaving of African and non-African ideas both of form and content but also, underlying this, an inexhaustible spring of native originality and creative impulse. Applied to any other great tradition this might seem banal, for where is the major culture that stands uniquely on its own? But with Africa the comment is not banal, or not yet, for we have only begun to give Africa its just weight and value in the balance of cultural give and take. Outside influences have long been recognized, and recent archaeological finds have widened their possible scope and impact. It is easy, for example, to accept the view that Chinese styles in metalware became popular at Meroë, since the Kushites are known to have had many trading ties with the sailors of the Indian Ocean and therefore, in all likelihood, with Han China; while a number of bronze vessels lately recovered in eastern Nigeria have plausibly suggested that the Chinese note may have struck its distant echo even as far as West Africa. Yet, at the same time, we have underestimated the weight on the "native African" side of the scales. "I am more and more inclined," a well-known authority on African sculpture observed the other day, "to think that Egypt owed more to Negro Africa than the other way round."

Unity and maturity are evident, even emphatically so, in the cultural and artistic traditions of many African regions and periods. Along the great rivers of central and western Africa there were peoples whose outstanding skill in the carving of wood produced a wealth of individual styles, which were nonetheless impelled by a broad community of ideas and themes, itself the product, as we have seen, of a common historical experience. Out on the high veld of the central southern plateau, where strong states and empires came to life in medieval times, stone ruins now begin to yield a coherent pattern of development over a prolonged period. The mythical Phoenicians said to have built Zimbabwe (see page 57), greatest of all these many sites, have been banished from the scene: once again the African side of the balance has acquired a new weight. Thus the site of Zimbabwe is now known to have been occupied by a succession of Iron Age peoples through more than a thousand years; and the walls of that strange "temple," as they may be seen today, were built by Africans at about the same time that the *Mayflower* breasted the Atlantic.

These peoples of the high veld were mining gold and selling it to eastern traders as early as the tenth century. They worked extensively in metals, sometimes with remarkable results. Plate-gold fragments of a sceptre and small rhinoceros figures from the site of Mapungubwe in the northern Transvaal are thinner than five-thousandths of an inch, witness to a rare degree of preindustrial skill. Even in the ruined medieval cities of the east coast, where Arabian influence was strong and venerable, Islamic architecture is seen to have acquired a distinctive style of its own. There, too, Swahili poetry touched lyrical and epic greatness.

Today a new Africa confronts the world, independent, resurgent, claiming a place of dignity and due respect in the councils of men. No doubt it may be high time for the rest of us to look at this claim with the eye of understanding, and for that a reassessment of African culture will be essential.

The English novelist and reporter Basil Davidson has himself done much to awaken interest in African history, through books like The Lost Cities of Africa *(1959) and* Black Mother *(1961).*

Whatever Became of Personal Ethics?

Out of fashion, tainted with snobbery and caste, the code of private honor needs renewal

By LOUIS KRONENBERGER

In today's business and professional world, which employs the educated, the clever, the gifted—a world of air waves and advertising copy, of publicity and promotion, of newsprint and coated stock, of regional distribution and national circulation—great numbers of those recruited espouse a certain political and social philosophy. They are liberals. They have liberal objectives, vote liberal tickets, support liberal causes. They are genuinely social-minded; are unreservedly for integration, slum clearance, socialized medicine, prison reform; for old-age benefits and reclaimed young delinquents; for due process, for free speech, for abolishing censorship. Some are violent about Southerners, some about Communists, some about Catholics. Some think practicality the most workable idealism, others fear that power corrupts, whatever its character. Some, worn out by the long grind, grow more militant in their liberalism; others, perked up by the new promotion, grow more perfunctory. But they are all liberals in no very ambiguous sense, on no quickly satirized terms.

Most of them, indeed, practice what they preach, not only in the voting booth but at the town meeting, in the books they buy, the warm-potato injustices they protest, and only a little less than formerly in the schools where they enroll their children. They firmly believe in the future. *Future,* as it happens, is the key word, the complicating word. For their own future marches, side by side as it were, with mankind's. Or rather, it fails to march side by side, from forever jockeying for position, jostling for precedence. For these, after all, are the big futurity stakes, this is the mammoth rat-race purse, and *their* future can on occasion be at odds with mankind's. How bravely wave the banners of progress! How meanly read the interoffice directives!

The schism these liberals have made between the self and society has somewhat the nature of a deal. The basis of the deal is not to hamper the self *in* society, not to allow one's social ideals to impede one's personal welfare. Character, that is to say, must not stand in the way of career; belief must not always govern behavior. In a sense, of course, the new schism is as old as the human race; is the eternal clash between our acquisitive instincts and our aspiring ones, between the thrust of ambition and the prick of conscience. But in another sense there is perhaps something truly new about

this schism—something that is both new and contradictory.

People who in the past led lives of educated careerism seldom espoused militantly social-minded aims. They often showed a proper community spirit, or denounced political corruption in their own backyards; they did much for growing children and something for wayward girls, they favored hospitals and settlement houses, they supported orchestras and art museums. But they seldom gave vocal support to social programs that reached beyond personal benevolence and private charity. They righted wrongs as against affirming rights; they did not plump for a social progress that might threaten their own. *Political* opportunists may have done so; or crusaders like the New England abolitionists who, as mill owners, were exploiters as well. But few business careerists have been open—and purse-open—liberals, rejecting all the arguments of a reasoned conservatism and hailing a future that should redress the wrongs of the past. What they alone except from all this is the present. The present may require their groveling before the boss, or being a touch treacherous toward a colleague, or taking credit for someone else's bright idea, or transferring the blame for one's own mistake; it may require whooping up the network's clownish censorship or craven cancellations; it may demand a little polite job-lifting or sabotage or slander. But if it does, that springs from bondage to today's dog-eat-dog world and man-bites-man methods, and is in strong contrast to the forward-march into the future, to the crusade against all repression that doesn't obstruct promotion.

The new careerists are a sort of debased intellectual class who, by way of their knowledge and skill, have become rather the mouthpieces and writing-hands of business than outright businessmen. Careers, for them, are not usually a tower to climb to the very top of, but a tunnel to work their way through, with plump economic security at the other end. These people have sought no philosophy to glorify their actions, have seldom rationalized their liberalism to mesh it with their livelihoods. They haven't even, a great many of them, turned hard: they are simply hardened to their roles and resigned to what they entail, not least to New Dealing, as it were, from the bottom of the deck.

And this means, as I have said, that in terms of liberal

objectives, wherever possible, they practice what they preach. Moreover, it is often possible—they can help their fellow-man wherever he is segregated or jailed or flogged, censored or silenced, slum-dwelling or dispossessed. They only cannot when he is their colleague or competitor, their friend or peer. And this seems new to me—a dog-eat-dog careerism that crusades for the underdog. These people do steadily, quite early in life, what the hard-fisted rich used to do very late: they pay conscience money. But today's, unlike yesterday's, is not paid retroactively in leisured remorse; it is pay-as-you-go penance.

Along with this, there has resulted something I don't want to exaggerate but that, taking even the most moderate view, seems extremely disquieting. There has resulted, among far too many intelligent and educated people, the complete substitution of social morality for personal ethics. To some extent, this may come of their taking personal ethics for granted; or of their assuming that as social morality advances, personal ethics must also. But I suspect that it measurably derives from something else—from a feeling that personal ethics, as a specific exhortation, reeks of both copybook maxims and conservative class thinking.

The phrase "personal honor" so smacks of code that a dozen years ago one shied away from it, a generation ago even tended to mock it. One would still prefer a phrase like "personal decency"; but the two are not the same, and it is perhaps the very idea of code that now weighs in honor's favor. For the decent man largely *lacks* the prejudices that becloud social vision; the honorable man behaves well in spite of having them.

What was too often amiss with personal honor was its restricting itself to a group or a class or a nation, rather than embracing humanity at large; was its becoming, at its worst, the Southern-gentleman or old-school-tie kind of thing. But, purged of class limitations, it remains a final touchstone of conduct—first, from its governing regardless of personal bias, from its operating toward enemy no less than friend; and again, from its being born of inner pride and self-respect. To take unfair advantage or use ungenerous means shamed oneself; and on this score at least—of its creating no guilt or self-contempt—it made for a healthier society, or at least a healthier basis for one. Personal honor, to be sure, often rested on dishonorably gained wealth, and could constitute a kind of luxury ideal. But it actually operated, and still operates, among *all* classes, in all sorts of communities; where it all too little operates today is in the intelligent, educated world I am speaking of.

Well, we need not bring back the phrase with its unwelcome overtones of caste; "personal ethics" will do very nicely. But, observing the steep decline of the thing itself in a "liberal" society, we must bring back some phrase to express it. Think just of pure surface manifestations today—think of the pokes and sideswipes among all sorts of news personalities, and in columns, and on the air; think of the snideness and malice, in public, of all sorts of "superior"

people, self-righteous intellectuals no less than self-seeking entertainers. Liberals, almost every one of them. Many of them may be nothing more than decidedly touchy and pushy; others nothing worse than compulsively opportunist; doubtless only one in five is really adept at character assassination or at knife-in-the-back. Broadway, for example, abounds in social-minded, cause-conscious people; Broadway resists reaction, opposes censorship; but Broadway provides a proverbially well-lighted stage for the envenomed ego and the venal claw.

A frequent defense among the opportunists is that their jettisoning of ethics is not cynical, but deterministic. It is a matter of "up or out"; even should you not breathe down the neck of the man ahead of you, the man behind is breathing down yours. Certainly there is truth in all this, not least in that the rat race is now an obstacle race as well; if you don't win a prize, you must pay a forfeit.

All that I have said, it must surely be clear, has no more to do with attacking liberalism than decrying Sunday Christianity has to do with attacking faith. The morality involved, it seems to me, can be worse than conscience-money morality; can be pure escapist morality, and escapist in two ways. For, however real these people's sympathy with the diverse victims of society, the fact remains that such victims nowhere impinge on these people's world, nowhere threaten it. And there is the second fact that toward all such victims these people can feel a *beneficent* guilt, a wholly impersonal guilt, for the wrongs done here are done by others, where the wrongs done closer to home all too often are not. To protest one kind of misbehavior while indulging in another is all too familiar; here, coming from people who so much shape present-day conduct, it can be all too dangerous as well.

If the relatively high-placed and influential indulge more and more in methods that shrug off personal ethics, must not such methods come before long to be regarded everywhere as normal? Won't we, rather than abolishing the rat race, have simply made it available to everybody? Already there exist television spokesmen for liberalism whose programs get gossipy and personal and who, while enjoying large incomes from the programs, pay their panelists nothing. Already there are Broadway big shots whose social ideas seem sound enough but who can behave like monsters. Already we have newspapers that, under the guise of being humanely broad-minded about what disturbs and distorts people, exploit every humiliating, distorting detail. What price equality when intelligent human beings claw one another for a foot-and-three-eighths of precedence, or for billing half an inch larger?

By all means let us extend, wherever possible, every form of social endeavor. But how ultimately great is the gain to bring up children with no prejudice against race and with every sympathy for the poor, if they are to have no scruples against back-stabbing, and an utter apathy toward fair play?

Louis Kronenberger, essayist, author of Company Manners *(among other books), and former theatre critic of* Time *magazine, is visiting professor of English at Stanford University.*

By PETER QUENNELL

In the Glow of the Perfect Patron

Lord Egremont's

whims included art and artists, and Turner painted luminous works at Petworth for him

One autumn morning in 1826 an uncommonly gifted writer, who, with far less justification, imagined that he was a great artist, awoke to congratulate himself on his good fortune. Benjamin Robert Haydon, author of the famous *Autobiography* and a painter of enormous disjointed historical scenes with titles like *Alexander Taming Bucephalus*, or *Wellington Musing at Waterloo*, had recently been the inhabitant of a debtors' prison, "the companion of gamblers and scoundrels—sleeping in wretchedness and dirt, on a flock bed low and filthy." He now opened his eyes beneath the canopy of a velvet-curtained four-poster and saw an array of splendid ancestral portraits glimmering through the shadows of the room. He was at Petworth, he remembered, the guest of a millionaire patron of contemporary art: "God in heaven [he exclaimed] grant my future may now be steady. At any rate a nobleman has taken me by the hand,

Under the Earl of Egremont's patrimony, the splendid estate of Petworth in Sussex (left) became an artistic haven frequented over many decades by Turner, whose 1831 water color Interior *(above) records a moment in one of the great house's rooms.*

63

The sumptuous Grinling Gibbons Room at Petworth is named for the celebrated sculptor whose carvings embellish its walls

The third Earl of Egremont

J. M. W. Turner

On the following pages HORIZON *presents a selection of Turner's Petworth water colors painted on blue-gray paper in and around the home of Lord Egremont, who befriended and encouraged the artist for almost thirty fruitful years, from 1809 until Egremont's death in 1837. Inside Petworth House, Turner's paintings held favored places; the walls of the Red Room alone were given over entirely to thirteen of his large canvases. Turner's prodigious lifetime output, which includes more than twenty thousand oils, water colors, and drawings, ranges from the almost literal draftsmanship of his early works to the blazing indefiniteness of his later ones, with their masses of primary color—unmixed blues, reds, and yellows. The series of water colors executed by Turner at Petworth may be regarded as preparation for the oil masterpieces to come—Venice; The Fighting Temeraire; Rain, Steam and Speed—yet each one shows his deepening appreciation of the nature of light, its interpenetration of air, and its fusion with the objects it envelops. Painting with a sharpened personal vision and economy, Turner illuminates a tree as though from within, a margin of lake reeds, a cluster of figures in a room, or a bank of sun-touched clouds above a skyline.*

whose friendship generally increases in proportion to the necessity of its continuance. Such is Lord Egremont."

Around the house stretched the immense, magnificently landscaped park and the long artificial lake that had already provided Turner with some of his most enchanting subjects. For Lord Egremont had many other protégés, whom he encouraged to treat his house as an artistic caravansary, and whose pictures he was fond of purchasing to set off his collection of old masters. He was naturally generous; and he could afford to be generous, having succeeded to an earldom when he was twelve years old, and with it inherited an income of more than £200,-000 per annum. He could also afford to be eccentric and made full use of his opportunities. Born in 1751, the friend and schoolfellow of Charles James Fox, he had entered the London world under the aegis of the dissolute Prince of Wales, and for some years had divided his time between politics, fashion, racing, and the improvement of his vast estates. "Had he chosen [we are told] he might have taken a conspicuous part in politics." But Egremont did not choose—he was either too lazy or too independent; nor did he choose to settle down in marriage with some suitably rich and wellborn girl. He suffered, his critics alleged, from "indiscretion and irresolution." What was more, he had fallen under the spell of a fashionable London beauty—Lady Melbourne, later Byron's confidante, whose second son, William Lamb, afterwards Queen Victoria's first Prime Minister, was widely believed to be Lord Egremont's illicit offspring. Her portrait, painted by Joshua Reynolds—a shrewd, sensuous, seductive face—now hangs in the room at Petworth that was once his bedchamber.

As the century approached its close, Egremont's interests veered toward art; but whereas his father, the second Earl, had begun to enlarge the family collection when traveling on the Grand Tour and had brought home some fine Italian paintings, he himself was chiefly attracted by the productions of the modern English school. Then, early in the new century, he became Turner's patron and personal friend; and their friendship, despite every kind of superficial difference, lasted until his death. Egremont was a hereditary grandee with (Joseph Farington once complained) "a great deal of the Peer about him," while Turner, the son of a miserly London barber, had inherited his

*I*n Park Scene with Figures *Turner's light brush evokes the mellow scenery of Petworth's glades and woods*

*L*ord Egremont Remembered: *"Solid, liberal, rich and English"*

"At dinner [Egremont] meets everybody, and then are recounted the feats of the day. All principal dishes he helps, never minding the trouble of carving; he eats heartily and helps liberally. There is plenty, but not absurd profusion; good wines, but not extravagant waste. Everything solid, liberal, rich and English. At seventy-four he still shoots daily, comes home wet through, and is as active and looks as well as many men of fifty.

"The meanest insect at Petworth feels a ray of his Lordship's fire in the justice of its distribution.

"I never saw such a character, or such a man, nor were there ever many. . . .

"Lord Egremont is dead; a great loss to all, especially artists. He was an extraordinary man—manly, straightforward, tender-hearted, a noble patron, an attached friend and an affectionate and indulgent parent. His great pleasure was in sharing with the highest and humblest the advantages and luxuries of his vast income. The very animals at Petworth seemed happier than in any other spot on earth, better fed, and their dumbness and helpless dependence on man more humanely felt for. He was one of those left of the old school who considered a great artist as fit society for any man, however high his rank, and at his table, as at Sir George Beaumont's, Lord Mulgrave's, or Sir Robert Peel's, painter and sculptor, poet and minister and soldier, all were as equals."*

—from Benjamin Robert Haydon's Autobiography

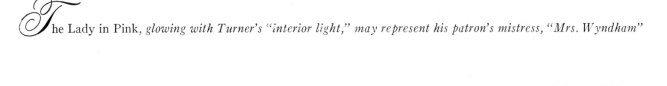

parent's miserliness—"Dad," he recorded, "never praised me except for saving a shilling"—and made no attempt to cut a gentlemanly figure. We hear of him at Petworth in 1809, when he resembled a prosperous "master carpenter, with lobster-red face, twinkling, staring gray eyes, white tie, blue coat with brass buttons . . . turned-up boots, large fluffy hat and enormous umbrella." And in the following year he is described as a "little Jewish-nosed man in an ill-cut brown coat, striped waistcoat, and . . . frilled shirt, sketching on a small piece of paper, held almost level with his waist." His private life was sordid and complex, occupied with a strange succession of clandestine love affairs. Now he would vanish among the brothels and taverns of London's dockside East End; now, as "Admiral Puggy Booth," he would be discovered living incognito in a secluded house with one of his various middle-aged favorites.

Yet eccentric responded to eccentric. Beneath the social carapace, painter and patron were human beings of much the same stamp: both shy, proud, and *farouche*, both impatient of accepted codes—Egremont because he was an aristocrat born, Turner because he was a man of genius. Each framed his own

laws and went his individual way. Thus the nobleman, who had refused to marry a debutante, lived for many years in domestic concubinage with an unpretentious young woman called Miss Iliffe. Some believed her father was a clergyman, others that he was a farmer; and it was said she had lived under Lord Egremont's protection since the age of fifteen. But she had adopted his family name, was known as "Mrs. Wyndham," lived at Petworth (though she did not dine with her lover when he entertained important persons), and bore him six illegitimate children—three sons and three daughters—who, unlike their retiring mother, seem to have attended all his parties. Mrs. Wyndham, too, was interested in the arts; and among the artists she encouraged was the wild visionary William Blake. Alas, the time came when Lord Egremont at length announced that he would marry her. The result was tragic: she grew unreasonably jealous. Marriage was soon followed by separation; and she was dismissed to occupy a comfortable house in London.

Meanwhile visiting artists continued to come and go, often with their wives and families. Petworth, wrote the celebrated diarist Charles Greville, resembled in its heyday "a great inn. Every-

body came when they thought fit, and departed without notice or leave-taking." Lord Egremont had a horror of farewell ceremonies and merely expected that his visitors should enjoy themselves. "Live and let live," observed Haydon, appeared to be his motto: "At breakfast . . . in walks Lord Egremont; first comes a grandchild whom he sends away happy. Outside the window moan a dozen black spaniels, who are let in, and to them he distributes cakes and comfits. . . . After chatting with one guest, and proposing some scheme of pleasure to others, his leathern gaiters are buttoned on, and away he walks. . . ." But his restlessness was always remarkable, whatever the company and wherever he happened to be. "He never remained," says Greville, "for five minutes in the same place, and was continually oscillating between the library and his bedroom, or wandering about the enormous house in all directions; sometimes he broke off in the middle of a conversation on some subject which appeared to interest him and disappeared, and an hour after, on a casual meeting, would resume it just where he had left off."

Physically an imposing personage, with a large head and handsome, high-nosed Roman features that suggested a more patrician version of Turner's rugged aquiline mask, Egremont had a correspondingly impressive mind—an "acute understanding," declared the diarist Thomas Creevey, and "much more knowledge . . . than he chuses to pretend to, and which he never discloses but incidentally, and, as it were, by compulsion. Simplicity and sarcasm are his distinguishing characteristics." This was in 1828. He did not die until 1837, and in 1832, when he celebrated his eighty-first birthday, we learn that he was "still healthy, with faculties and memory apparently unimpaired"; while in 1834 he gave a memorable fete for six thousand of the poor from surrounding areas, who sat down to feast at an *al fresco* banquet on mountains of plum puddings and "innumerable joints of boiled and roast beef." Nothing could have exceeded their host's enjoyment as he rode round among the crowded tables. According to Greville, who was among those present, it was "one of the gayest and most beautiful spectacles" that he had ever seen.

The background of the fete was Petworth House, and few collectors and men of taste have inherited a more appropriate

M orning in the open: a cool Turneresque mist hovers about the restless group of horses and hunters gathering for a meet

setting. Once the home of Henry Percy, the "Wizard Earl" of Northumberland, scientist and patron of learning in the reigns of Elizabeth I and James I, it had passed through the female line to another powerful nobleman, "The Proud Duke" of Somerset. Somerset pulled down the medieval and Tudor buildings and, about 1688, with the help of an architect-sculptor who may possibly have come from France—Pierre Puget, known in England as "the French Michelangelo," is among the names that have been suggested—started to construct and embellish the present western façade, incorporating decorative motifs that recall the designs of Daniel Marot. The Earl of Northumberland had employed Van Dyck to paint a series of brilliant family portraits; Somerset commissioned Louis Laguerre to decorate the main staircase and engaged Grinling Gibbons, the renowned woodcarver, to produce his masterpiece, "The Carved Room" (see page 64), which he festooned with delicate filigree garlands of leaves and flowers, fruit and fluttering birds, horns of plenty, coronets and ducal insignia, musical instruments, classical vases, and kissing and trumpet-blowing *putti*.

Into this sumptuous receptacle, further dignified by the for-

eign paintings that the second Earl had purchased on his Grand Tour, Lord Egremont inserted the English collection that he had begun to accumulate during the late eighteenth and early nineteenth centuries. It includes the works of Reynolds, Gainsborough, Romney, and Hoppner; and both Romney and Hoppner painted large groups of the owner's blooming illegitimate children. Egremont's taste was not invariably sound—he was a cultured dilettante rather than an expert critic; and, besides paintings we still admire today, we find the second- or third-rate productions of Northcote, Angelica Kauffmann, Haydon (in whom the purchaser's interest may have been partly charitable), Harlow, Clint, the anecdotal Leslie, and the neo-classical sculptor John Flaxman. Clearly, Egremont liked a "clever" picture and was not averse to a picture that told a story. On the other hand, he was by no means conservative; and either he or Mrs. Wyndham—to whom the poet-painter once dedicated some characteristic verses—bought Blake's vision of *Hell and Paradise* and a panel, painted on the front and the back, by that mysterious Anglo-Swiss artist Henry Fuseli, the only man, according to Blake, who did not make him "almost spew." Nor

*L*ord Egremont and his guests, summed up by Turner in swift splashes of color, wait for the dinner gong

was Constable neglected: he visited Petworth in 1834 and came away with a large notebook filled with pencil drawings and water-color sketches.

But it is for the friendship he extended to Turner that this grandiose eccentric will always be best remembered. So scrupulously did Egremont respect the painter's moods that he built him a studio in a convenient upper room, and agreed never to cross its threshold without giving a prescribed knock. Turner's first visit was paid in 1809; in 1810 he produced *Petworth House from the Lake, Dewy Morning,* painted from a point of view that can still be recognized, though Turner later added some inappropriate fishing smacks; and in 1830 or thereabouts his friend acquired that strikingly original painting *Jessica,* a symphony of green and gold and rose and black, with Shakespeare's heroine in a modern plumed hat looking through an open casement. Not only did Turner paint the park, he frequently painted the interior of the house—sometimes in a shimmering blaze of color, as in his impressionistic *Drawing Room, Petworth,* now at London's National Gallery; sometimes in a series of rapid impressions, like the tiny luminous sketch, preserved at Petworth, that

shows one of Lord Egremont's female relations impatiently sponging her blue silk dress, after the awkward and embarrassed painter, while eating his breakfast, had somehow managed to upset a cream jug.

If Petworth and its surroundings inspired Turner, he seems himself, in some occult fashion, to have quickened and enriched the spirit of the landscape. Today, when the sun climbs over the lake and the rolling wooded hills beyond, or when the evening light grazes the burnished surface of the grass and picks out a group of dappled fallow deer, their antlers faintly tipped with gold, at rest beneath a distant tree, the effect is so perfectly "Turneresque" that we feel that we must have entered his imaginary world—the world of an artist who loved light and believed that light was a manifestation of God; indeed, that the sun *was* God, as he is said to have whispered in his last recorded utterance.

Peter Quennell, the distinguished biographer and essayist, has written studies of Byron, Hogarth, and Ruskin, and is co-editor of the magazine History Today.

The lake at Petworth has changed little since it was painted by Turner a century and a quarter ago

From Eden to the Nightmare

By HENRY ANATOLE GRUNWALD

Dissatisfied with the world as it exists, men have always tried to imagine the world as it might become. Time, though, has darkened their utopian visions in more ways than one

Utopia has almost always been somewhere on the map of man's imagination. Every age, with some notable exceptions, has created a realm of Nowhere for its visions of the future. The frontiers of this realm are not precise. It should not be confused with Arcadia or the Golden Age, that space-time continuum (as we might put it) in which life was good and innocent; these dreams lie in the past. Nor is it the same as the land of Cockaigne or the Schlaraffenland of German legend, where roast fowl offer themselves up ready for the eating, where every prospect pleases and not even man is vile; those regions are merely playthings of fancy. Nor is Utopia the same as the Messianic Kingdom, where, in the words of the prophet, "the wolf also shall dwell with the lamb, and the leopard shall lie down with the kid . . . and the lion shall eat straw like the ox." For that peaceable kingdom, though it may be located on earth, can come about only through divine intervention.

Utopia is a city of man. Yet in their own way the utopians were prophets in the sense of predicting the future and also prophets in the sense of castigating the present; their very vision of things as they should be was a reproach to things as they are.

One of the extraordinary facts about our time is that its utopias are dark. They are no longer places of hope but of horror, no longer heaven on earth but hell on earth. How this happened is suggested by Nicolas Berdyaev, in a passage that Aldous Huxley used as his epigraph to *Brave New World:* "Utopias can be realized. Life is marching toward utopias. And perhaps a new century is beginning in which the intellectuals and the cultured classes will dream about means of evading utopia and of returning to non-utopian society, less 'perfect,' but freer."

In the past the triumphs of science led us to *hubris.* Today even greater scientific triumphs have led, on the whole, to fear. We can scarcely manage this world, we seem to feel; how are we to manage others? We have come to deride and deplore the Victorian era's unshakable optimism about man's destiny.

This involves a paradox, because in some respects we are still the heirs of Rousseau and of the Enlightenment, which held man to be essentially good and perfectible. This notion is reflected in our sociology and psychology, in our belief that good environment will make good people, that wrongdoing can be cured almost like a disease. And yet at the same time, with another part of our minds, we don't accept all this. We have seen too much blood and horror in this century, too much tampering with the "environment," too much "conditioning," too much "adjustment," ever again to feel easy about any attempt to achieve human perfection—and utopia is nothing if not a dream of conditioning, of environment wisely controlled.

Constructing a utopia used to be a fairly simple process. You substituted peace for war, altruism for selfishness, temperance for greed, love for hate. Today we do not turn the world upside down, we simply take it as it is and make it more so. The result is almost invariably nightmarish. In a recent address Huxley declared that "there are the near-in utopias, where

The first utopia was the Garden of Eden, but since no man knows what Eden was like, anyone may re-create it in his own image. Hieronymus Bosch, who about 1500 painted his triptych The Garden of Earthly Delights *(opposite), saw it as a place of marvels untinged by his own world's reality.*

73

N. Y. PUB. LIB. RARE BOOK DIV.

people like ourselves have solved their social and psychological problems in ways which to us are unfamiliar. And there are the far-out utopias, inhabited by creatures unlike ourselves—creatures whose problems are either nonexistent or so different from ours as to seem irrelevant." Past utopias, Huxley continued, were all intended to be positive, "but in every case an oversimplified view of human nature, combined with the lust for tidiness . . . has reversed the sign and transformed these ideal states into negative utopias which, in spite of their authors' underlying good will and sporadic good sense, are potentially as horribly inhuman as Orwell's *1984.*" To see how this came about we must begin with Plato's *Republic,* the prototype utopia of them all.

What disturbs us about *The Republic* is quite simply the fact that Plato was more interested in order than in liberty. We feel that, when it comes to the people, the whole is greater than the part; individually they may be ignorant, but collectively they are wise. To Plato, of course, this notion would have been wicked nonsense. At best the people at large, like the false philosophers, might be capable of "opinion," which he considered an intermediate stage between knowledge and ignorance. The mob was merely "the great brute," and its rule could only be brutish. Not that in his view the common people are necessarily wicked or intractable. They are like children who must be led, and when necessary lied to, for their own good. "Our rulers," he says, "will have to administer a great quantity of falsehood and deceit for the benefit of the ruled."

As for the practical organization of the Republic, it is a city-state of strictly limited size; the optimum number of citizens Plato held to be 5,040, approximately the number of people who could be reached on a single occasion by a single orator before the time of public-address systems, radio, and television. The people are divided into Plato's famous metallic class structure, the rulers, or guardians, being symbolically composed of gold, the auxiliaries, or soldiers, of silver, and the workers of brass and iron. But there is a certain amount of mobility. "A golden parent will sometimes have a silver son, or a silver parent a golden son."

This mobility is aided by abolition of the family, at least among the ruling class. Theoretically all women are the wives of all men. At special festivals mating is arranged by lot, but only among partners judged likely to produce healthy offspring. Children are taken from their mothers at birth, and reared by the state. Thus there will be no private family feeling to detract from love and loyalty to the Republic. Nor is there any private property. This is particularly important for the guardians, for if they owned land and houses privately, they would become hateful masters rather than fatherly friends to the people.

The muses, like everyone else, are in the service of Plato's ideal state. Artists and writers are silenced or severely censored. Nevertheless, one finds in *The Republic,* as one is pushed on through the almost hypnotically reasonable interchanges, a serenity and clarity that are hard to resist. There is also a bucolic yearning that characterizes most utopias before the advent of technology, often remarkably naïve and detailed. The people will "produce corn, and wine, and clothes, and shoes, and build houses for themselves . . . they will work, in summer, commonly, stripped and barefoot, but in winter substantially clothed and shod. They will feed on barley-meal and flour of wheat, baking and kneading them, making noble cakes and loaves. . . ."

The underlying view of justice, of which the Republic is but a civic incarnation, is simply this: each in his own place and station, each performing his proper function, each minding his own business. Needless to say, with the exception of some lowlier matters that are not worth his while, the philosopher's business is to mind everybody's.

In various combinations, and with changing emphasis, most of these Spartan ingredients reappear in virtually all utopias after Plato. While we might conceivably tolerate the loss of property, privacy, family, and art, what truly makes Plato's Republic unacceptable to us, as democrats, is the notion of an infallible elite. What is unanswered in *The Republic* and in most other utopias is the immortal question: Who guards the guardians?

Plato and many other utopians can only present more or less impressive schemes for the guardians' education and training; they can only base their structures on the tautology that the wise man is wise. In few of the utopias is there a real check on the rulers; there cannot be, for everything depends on their goodness and wisdom. Plato was somewhat naïve about the nature of power, as are so many other utopians. He condemned tyranny, but did he fully understand what tempts men to become tyrants? Did he understand that a philosopher, once given power, might be so gripped by the passion for establishing the truth, his truth, that he would start working out his syllogisms in human lives? What troubles us, then, is not the notion that the philosopher should be king, but the serene assumption that a philosopher will never be a tyrant.

For nearly two thousand years after Plato, utopia almost never appeared on the map. Christianity looked to the City of God. Throughout the long Christian centuries until the Renaissance, mankind was taught not to yearn for heaven on earth; heaven itself seemed too close and too real. Only when the Christian vision of paradise began to lose its hold was it time once again to long for a secular paradise. It is surely no accident that Sir Thomas

More's *Utopia* is, fictionally, a by-product of the intoxicating age of discoveries; for its narrator professes to have been a sailing companion of Amerigo Vespucci and to have found his happy island in the New World.

Following the lead of *The Republic,* More abolishes private property in Utopia. Since there is no property, there is no money. The citizens of Utopia just go to the nearest district storehouse and draw what they need. This material abundance More imagined as being created simply by the fact that everyone works—princes, rich men, would-be idlers. They toil but six hours a day, a condition that only a few of today's most ambitious trade unions have as yet achieved for their members. Besides, More established a kind of circular economic law: since there is enough for everybody, no one hoards; and since no one hoards, there is enough for everybody.

This seems a rather naïve way of doing away with greed, for it assumes that greed is caused only by the fear of want. In the matter of what he called "pomp and excess" More was equally simple. Precious metals are despised in his Utopia. Gold is used to make chamber pots and the chains of slaves. Pearls are playthings for children.

Unlike Plato, More was all for the family. It forms the basic social unit of Utopia, but it is subject to a good deal of regulation. Divorce is permitted for adultery, or insufferable perverseness, as well as by mutual consent for other causes, provided the government approves. While men and women are free to mate more or less as they please, care must be taken to prevent mistakes. The physical soundness of both parties must be ascertained and they must view each other naked before marriage.

Liberty was not the ideal in Utopia, any more than in the Republic. The ideal was stability. Like Plato, More considered the institution of slavery indispensable, if only to get the meaner jobs in life done. And, like most utopians after him, he had a touch of agoraphobia—particularly strange for a Renaissance man—in the sense that he yearned for the smallish, well-secluded corner of the world. In addition to this desire for seclusion, More set some other fashions for later utopians. Like most of them, he was preoccupied with sanitation. Like most of them, he called for as few laws as possible, and banished lawyers from the state. And like most of them, he had a passion for ceremonial and housekeeping details. But unlike many of his successors, More faced up to the matter of war and proposed that it should be waged by assassination of the enemy's leaders. Why kill so many in battle when a few well-chosen deaths might settle the issue?

More was far easier than Plato on the arts, music, and pleasure in general. He considered it to be man's natural goal in life, but he distinguished between higher and lower, worthier and un-

LIBRARY OF CONGRESS

worthier pleasures. While not spurning food, drink, or the feeling "which arises from satisfying the appetite which Nature has wisely given to lead us to the propagation of the species," he ranks as the highest pleasure of all cultivation of the mind. This is made abundantly clear even at mealtime, to which citizens are summoned by trumpet calls. All meals are taken in common in vast dining halls, on the doubtful theory that no one would want to go to the bother of preparing his own meal at home when it is so easily available in a kind of super soup kitchen. All meals are begun "with some lecture of morality that is read to them," and for educational purposes the young are placed next to the old, so that the old men may "take occasion to entertain those about them with some useful and pleasant enlargements." Whatever can be said for life in Utopia, one would scarcely want to dine there.

For a hundred years after More there was no sign of significant new utopias. Then, within a few years of each other in the 1620's, three visions of ideal commonwealths appeared, and together they reflected some major new forces that were stirring the age. All three were to some extent preoccupied with science, invention, and manufacture.

The best known of the three is Francis Bacon's fragmentary *New Atlantis.* It offers a suitably exotic and isolated location, wise rulers, and a well-regulated family life. But above all, New Atlantis is imbued with its era's almost vernal passion for science. Here it is no longer the philosopher who is king, but the scientist. It is the kind of realm that might have been dreamed, with due allowance for the intervening centuries, by the head of a large, modern, state university; or perhaps it is really the Rockefeller Foundation transported to Utopia. At the heart of New Atlantis is Salomon's House, a vast research institution whose aim is to find "the knowledge of causes and secret motion of things; and the enlarging of the bounds of human empire, to the effecting of all things possible." The Salomon Foundation, as one is tempted to think of it, has agents roaming the earth (traveling research fellows?) looking for new discoveries, and it tries to examine almost anything the seventeenth-century mind can imagine.

If New Atlantis was the first scientific utopia, Christianopolis anticipates the first industrial one. Johann Valentin Andreae, a German Protestant scholar, dreamed of an "abode situated below the sky, but at the same time above the dregs of this known world." Part Platonic, part Calvinist, Christianopolis is made distinctive by its industrial organization. The whole community is in fact a workshop. With that geographic neatness which marks most utopian writers, Andreae sees his city as a square divided into three parts: one to supply food, one for drill and exercise, and one, disarmingly, for looks. The industrial sector, which is lo-

75

Until the mid-nineteenth century,
utopia was always positive; but then the
first negative ones began to appear,
such as the "Stahlstadt" of Jules Verne's
The Begum's Fortune *(1879). It*
was essentially a giant munitions factory
run like a concentration camp.

cated outside the city walls, is divided into manufactures requiring the use of fire and those that can be carried on without it—heavy and light industry in modern terms. The economic planner has made his entrance into utopia.

The third and most far-out in this trio of early seventeenth-century utopias is *The City of the Sun* by Tommaso Campanella, an Italian Dominican monk who believed in astrology and spent considerable time in the prisons of the Inquisition, where in fact he wrote his fantasy. It is a fascinating mixture of Platonic communism, Christian radicalism, Aztec custom, astrological speculation, technological anticipation, and scientific instinct. Both spiritual and temporal matters are in the hands of the high priest, known as Metaphysicus, who

BIB. D'EDUCATION ET RECREATION, PARIS

rules jointly with three associates and is described as the most staggeringly well-educated ruler in the visible and perhaps invisible world. Below this top level there is a hierarchy of magistrates all of whom are also priests; the entire population confesses its sins to them, and it is their duty to pardon them forthwith, while in turn confessing their own sins to their superiors—and so on up in a continuous confessional ascent.

Yet amid this eccentricity there is a certain grasp of reality and of the future. Despite all its quirks, The City of the Sun is remarkably sound on education, scientific inquiry, and hygiene. Labor has become dignified, and the slave class of so many earlier utopias has been discarded. And there is a heady belief in "the wonderful invention of printing and arquebuses, and the discovery of the use of the magnet." Strange as were Campanella's visions, they mark, with those of Andreae, a turning point. With them, as Lewis Mumford has said, "we stand at the entrance to the utopia of means; that is to say, the place in which all that materially contributes to the good life has been perfected."

The remainder of the seventeenth century brought a veritable blizzard of utopian or semi-utopian works, including *The Man in the Moone,* by Bishop Francis Godwin, and *Oceana,* by James Harrington. The latter, a strictly parliamentary paradise, was written in the days of Cromwell and is essentially a draft constitution, providing for division of lands and a balanced legislative system allowing the rule of "King People." It was one of the very few utopias concerned with the preservation of private property and individual liberty.

Beyond this, and until the end of the eighteenth century, there is a considerable void in utopian literature. Instead of plans for perfect commonwealths, the Age of Reason yearned for the primitive. Its utopia was the forest primeval with encyclopedias dangling from the trees. Chateaubriand dreamed of the noble savage and Rousseau proclaimed man to have been pure before society corrupted him. This belief in nature and man's natural goodness

was a strong radical force, since it seemed to justify razing the structures of society in order to start again from the ground up. Heightened to anarchic fervor, it fed the French Revolution. It also animated a group of oddly assorted idealists, by turns idyllic and radical, pacific and militant, democratic and tyrannical, who became known as the utopian Socialists. From the middle of the eighteenth century to the middle of the nineteenth, they drew up their schemes to tame the industrial revolution, until Karl Marx, sneering at their "unscientific" and vaporous dreams, began the movement that was to sweep them from the scene.

One of the first was Morelly (any other names, if he had them, are unknown), who is credited with originating the catch phrase, used with variations by most other socialists thereafter: "Each is to labor according to his ability and share according to his needs." Alarmingly liberal in some matters, Morelly felt that even incest should not be prohibited; authoritarian in other respects, he proposed that marriage should be compulsory, and that celibacy should be allowed only after the fortieth year.

More typical was Etienne Cabet, who in *Journey to Icaria* visualized, despite some romantic trimmings, a totally regimented community where the ideal of brotherhood is turned into the great relentless leveler. Since inequality of talent or intelligence is nature's fault, it is unjust to penalize the individual for it. Hence if some stand higher than others, they must be cut down to size; all dress alike, eat alike, learn alike, pray alike, and ultimately think alike. The environment is totally controlled: the city is laid out with mathematical precision, the sidewalks are covered against the rain, the streets are cleaned by special dust-collecting machines, and (Cabet shared the typical utopian's obsessive preoccupation with detail) the windows are designed to close noiselessly. People work for the state, love for the state, die for the state.

The most influential of the utopian Socialists was Charles Fourier, possibly because he approached utopia through psychology, though modern practitioners would scarcely recognize it as such. Human behavior, as he saw it, was a matter of the "passions" which, as we would put it today, had always been unduly repressed. They must be freed and harmonized with each other. In this he followed Rousseau and anticipated, however crudely, Freud. One cannot help wondering whether Freud's map of the psyche, with its division into id, ego, and superego, will a century hence seem as quaint as Fourier's map of the passions seems to us now. He counted twelve separate ones, from the "luxury" passions, corresponding to the five senses, to the "composite passion," or desire for union.

To harmonize all these passions, the proper environment is

William Morris's News from Nowhere
*(1890) looks forward to a time
(late in the twentieth century) when all
the dreams of nineteenth-century
socialism have come true. "Labour's
May-Day," the frontispiece of this
idealistic book, symbolizes its way of life.*

needed, and Fourier prescribed it in minute detail as the "phalanx," an association of about fifteen hundred people on a small unit of land, self-supporting through agriculture and light industry. Fourier was obviously trying to escape bigness—the bigness of modern industry, the bigness of modern state. But he foresaw a world federation of phalanxes under a Great Chief whose residence was to be, of all places, in Constantinople.

Private property was permitted subject to certain co-operative rules. Everyone within reason was to be free to choose the kind of work he wanted, and to switch if he got bored. A very similar arrangement was to apply to choosing mates. In short, Fourier visualized a utopia of free love. He predicted that if mankind adopted his plan, it would face a glorious future of seventy thousand years, when lions would not only eat straw but draw men's carriages, when whales would pull vessels and sea water would be turned into lemonade.

In one way Fourier was the most unfortunate of utopian thinkers, for people made a major and fatal attempt to put his ideas into practice. The experiments were carried out particularly in the United States during the 1840's, when hundreds of utopian "associations" sprang up, many of them directly inspired or influenced by Fourier.

One of the most typical experiments was Brook Farm. It was set up near Boston by two noted Unitarian clerics, George Ripley and Ellery Channing, to show among other things that work need not mean industrial degradation but could go hand in hand with joy, dignity, and culture. In part the idea was that intellectuals would perform physical labor in order to free laborers for intellectual pursuits. To the regret of the founders, Ralph Waldo Emerson refused to join; he had tried physical labor and decided that it was not ordained "that a writer should dig." Charles Dana stated Brook Farm's purpose simply: "Our ulterior aim is nothing less than Heaven on Earth." He added that "the practical result we first aim at is wealth," an aim that constantly eluded them. The Brook Farmers adopted Fourier with reservations, particularly concerning his sexual theories, but their reputation suffered. After all the press could scarcely ignore the fact, regardless of what conditions actually were at Brook Farm, that in his ideal communities Fourier had provided for the entertainment of men by "Corps of Bacchae and Bayadères."

Nathaniel Hawthorne, who later wrote about it in *The Blithedale Romance,* joined Brook Farm as director of agriculture, mostly in hopes that the settlement would prosper and make him solvent. He described it caustically as "a polar Paradise," and was highly uneasy about his farm chores, especially milking. He complained about one particularly mean cow, "a transcendental

ROBERTS BROS., BOSTON 1890

heifer belonging to Miss Margaret Fuller. She is very fractious, I believe, and apt to kick over the milk pail."

Brook Farm dissolved amid a series of financial misfortunes and fires, sharing the fate of another famous community of the period, Oneida. It had been founded in Putney, Vermont, by a sometime clergyman named John Humphrey Noyes, who in 1848 moved it to Oneida, New York. From the time he attended a seminary at Andover, Noyes had been striving to reach a life of Perfection—but had fluctuated between evangelical triumphs and sordid scandals, partly because he often tried to convert prostitutes and was seldom as successful with them as they were with him. On one occasion, he asked two respectable young ladies to come to bed with him in order to test their virtue; they flunked. At Oneida he developed a system of "complex marriage" based on the notion that the foundation of Christianity is the ultimate selflessness of sharing mates. Economically, the community flourished when it was joined by Sewall Newhouse, a manufacturer who made and sold steel springs. Earlier, men and women had been forbidden to have children. When the commune started showing a profit, Noyes at last gave his followers permission to have offspring. But childbearing in an aging free-love community could only lead to confusion, jealousy, heartbreak, and eventually scandal.

All the "association" utopias were inevitably doomed, not only because of their eccentric doctrines, their amateurish administration, and their sometimes questionable devotees, but because essentially they were trying to flee, or hide, from the reality of the machine age. Similar escape attempts occurred in literature until much later. In 1890 William Morris in his *News from Nowhere* dreamed of a new London that had become a cluster of villages amid idyllic woodlands, the only remnants from the past being the Houses of Parliament, now used to store dung. In 1887 W. H. Hudson gazed into the distant future to find *A Crystal Age,* in which society resolved itself into great country estates, each a little world with its own history and traditions, presided over by a housemother who is part goddess, part queen bee, and part Mom. Although these communities were theoretically set in the future, they were really dreams of the past.

The other, the forward-marching utopias were changing with the contemporary world that produced them. More and more industrialized, they were becoming, in Lewis Mumford's phrase, merely "vast reticulations of steel and red tape."

One of the earliest of these Utopias of Steel was, appropriately enough, Stahlstadt (Steel City), and it made its appearance in an 1879 book called *The Begum's Fortune* by Jules Verne. Built in Oregon by a wicked German planner named Dr. Schultz, Stahl-

One of H. G. Wells's many utopian
fantasies, When the Sleeper Wakes (1899)
is about a modern Rip Van Winkle
who awakens from a cataleptic trance in
a world where man has traded
freedom for security, all culture is canned,
and so is the climate (under domes).

stadt is one vast munitions plant whose workers are attached to the factory as medieval serfs were attached to the land. Verne was deliberately creating a negative utopia, but he also put a positive one in the same story. The significant thing is that the "good" utopia is scarcely more attractive to us than the "bad" one. It is a kind of germless garden city with identical brick houses on identical plots, where wallpaper and carpeting are forbidden, to guard against bacteria, and for the same reason the city's hospitals are burned down each year.

Something similar happened a few years later in *Looking Backward* when Edward Bellamy constructed his own Steel City, or rather, Steel State. It was intended as a positive utopia, but it seems the opposite to us. The entire population works for the state in a vast labor army, and in good utopian tradition all receive credit in return for their work and thus may draw what they need from great storehouses. No money, of course; no banks; no want; no crime—for, argued Bellamy, most crime is caused by "inequality of possessions." If supreme trust in a wise elite is the first great utopian fallacy, here is the second: the notion that men need only be drafted, as it were, and issued with decent rations to make them perfect.

Yet, for all his simple-mindedness, Bellamy was a chillingly accurate prophet, even if he did not understand the meaning of his prophecy. He foretold a lot that has become reality, from Muzak and piped-in religion to the labor army. In this sense *Looking Backward* is one of the most significant of all utopias, because it makes us see the all-important point: we used to deride utopia because it was unreal; now we dread it because it *is* real.

The belief that everything was possible to science, to the machine, was the great source of Victorian optimism, but there were dissenters. One of them was Samuel Butler, who in *Erewhon* had created perhaps the first full-scale negative utopia. He brilliantly satirized his age, by exaggerating—but less than even he realized—what was possible. We are today not very far removed from the Erewhonian notion that disease is a crime while crime is only a disease. Above all, we are remarkably close to his fantasy of the machine. Well over half a century before machines learned to "think," Butler visualized what would happen if they ever did. The fact that they still lacked consciousness, he warned, meant little; after all, a mollusc also lacked consciousness, but there were other species ahead. And as machines grow more human, man becomes more machinelike. The solution in *Erewhon* called for man to destroy the machine. Years later the outcome in Karel Čapek's *R.U.R.* would be the opposite: the machines destroyed man.

HARPER 1899

The Machine Triumphant is a theme that was carried on, not too long after Butler, by H. G. Wells, and to him it suggested both hope and horror, both promise and threat. Accordingly, his visions are both positive and negative. In *A Modern Utopia* he set out deliberately to discover what could be done with the old utopian traditions in a new age, and he broke with most of them. He abandons the usual yearning for smallness and seclusion by making his a world-wide community with a common language. He allows and indeed encourages both property and money, with some limitations. Above all, Wells is concerned with freedom, which he feels all previous utopias ignored or slighted. He favors neither individualism nor socialism but a mixture of the two, with the state looming large in everyone's life, but hardly more so than we are already accustomed to.

Wells's Platonic guardians, called samurai, are a large, voluntary, ruling aristocracy subject to a rigid code of behavior. They are forbidden games, alcohol, tobacco, servants, and dramatic religion—the faith of Utopia being a kind of syncretism the basis of which is the absence of original sin. The samurai must avoid anything that accustoms the mind to applause, and once a year they must spend a week in the wilderness, without books, money, or other amenities, in order to meditate. Altogether, Huxley may have been a trifle harsh when he remarked that the Wellsian samurai "think, feel and behave like a cross between the Boy Scouts and the Society of Jesus."

Huxley obviously would have preferred the earlier, or non-Boy Scout, Wells. In the last decade of the nineteenth century Wells took several bone-chilling looks into the future that add up to a formidably negative utopia, in sharp contrast to the urbane and engaging commonwealth he put together later. In *The Time Machine* he forecast a distant scene inhabited not by a race of supermen but by a tribe of childlike, soft creatures, the Eloi, descendants of our ruling classes whose vigor declined when the need for effort vanished. Underground, in the bowels of the earth, live the Morlocks, descendants of our proletariat, who from ancient habit run the machines needed for the comfort of the privileged, but who feed on the flesh of the Eloi whom they serve. Yet another vision of the future is "A Story of the Days to Come," which anticipates Huxley's own anti-utopia by several decades. In this brave new Wellsian world, advertising is bawled everywhere from loudspeakers, deviates have their antisocial traits removed by hypnosis, dreams can be obtained to order, education is offered by telephone, food is rendered synthetic and eaten

BALLANTINE BOOKS 1953

in automats, "face-molders" correct asymmetrical features, and in the end there is the Euthanasia Company always ready to be of service.

In *Men Like Gods,* written more than two decades later, Wells went to the opposite extreme and created a distinctly optimistic utopia, more or less based on evolution, which of course itself is one vast, biological utopia. In this positive mood Wells sees mankind as beginning to evolve toward a "nobler humanity, different in kind." While reading *Men Like Gods,* whose optimism revolted him thoroughly, Aldous Huxley decided to write a "derisive parody," a piece of "cynical anti-idealism" that eventually grew into *Brave New World.*

Huxley is to the negative or anti-utopia what Plato and More combined are to the positive. We are apt to be less familiar with the Republic's guardians and Utopia's jeweled toys than we are with Brave New World's Controllers, its hatched and identical humans, its sleep-conditioning, its feelies, its soma happy pills, and all the other paraphernalia of horror in the orgy-porgy of total organization. As Huxley himself has observed, mind control has become a reality in brain-washing, conditioning during sleep has been successfully attempted in experiments with sleep-teaching, Brave New World's mass pleasures that degrade and enslave the mind have their equivalent in our relentlessly distracting mass entertainment, and the soma pills of chemically induced happiness correspond to the millions upon millions of tranquilizers that our doctors prescribe every year.

Striking though these parallels are, it still takes a certain amount of straining to see *Brave New World* in our own. But it takes very little to see *1984.* George Orwell's masterpiece ranks, after *Brave New World,* as the greatest in the still somewhat specialized field of anti-utopias, and yet in a way it is not utopian at all. Big Brother and Doublethink are not, like the characters and devices of Huxley's work, cleverly extrapolated from the existing world; they *are* the existing world. They are what became of the Socialist utopia once it was subjected to Marx's "scientific" treatment. But how much ought we to blame on Marx, and how much was already present in those early revolutionary idylls and egalitarian schemes? The question must go even further back. For was not Big Brother born simultaneously with the Guardian, however noble of intent, ruling the Republic? And was not Doublethink invented with the principle that the people must be lied to for their own good?

The chief domain of Utopia today is science-fiction. The overwhelming majority of science-fiction utopias are negative, foreseeing a technologically supported totalitarianism. As is pointed out in Kingsley Amis's excellent *New Maps of Hell,* to which the following account is indebted, their villains are usually politicians or businessmen, rarely scientists or artists. These utopias generally reflect and warn against our present world by the device of horror caricature. Advertising, for instance, is the starting point for *The Space Merchants* by Frederik Pohl and C. M. Kornbluth, a kind of Madison Avenue anti-utopia where commercials can be projected directly on the retina, where Congressmen represent not states or districts but business firms. The consumer-oriented society is the starting point of the short story "The Midas Plague" also by Pohl, who visualizes an anti-utopia of glut in which mankind is flooded with goods. True comfort, true riches, consist in *not* having to consume more than one's neighbor. In "Null-P" by William Tenn, *homo abnegus,* totally mediocre man, has taken over and is eventually domesticated by a race of intelligent Newfoundland retrievers who prize him for his stick-throwing ability. In Ray Bradbury's *Fahrenheit 451* the hero is a fireman whose duties are systematically to burn proscribed books according to a fixed schedule: "Monday burn Millay, Wednesday Whitman, Friday Faulkner."

In these anti-utopias, the true hero is always man and whether or not he physically loses, his spirit is not broken. Yet this rebellion is almost never for a positive program. It simply seeks to restore human values. What the rebels want to establish in all these totalitarian nightmares seems to be, as Amis says, "a society just like our own, but with more decency and less television."

And that is basically where the matter of utopia rests today. Few, if any, serious writers attempt the form, and when they do, it is usually of the negative variety. That old negativist Aldous Huxley himself has recently attempted a positive utopia in his novel *Island,* with generally disastrous results.

A maverick intellectual, Paul Goodman, in his recent *Utopian Essays and Practical Proposals* put forth several ideas, including the notion that first-rate writers and composers be commissioned to provide a better ceremonial for public school commencements; that the loneliness of old-age homes and orphanages might be reduced by having old ladies take care of the orphans; and that private cars should be banned in New York City. While all these may be ingenious and possibly even sensible schemes (particularly the last one), it is strange to call them utopian as Goodman does. It suggests that in our time utopia has finally come down to the level of a traffic problem. Perhaps what we really want is eighteenth-century democracy with health insurance and lots of room to park. Our true utopia, it seems, is in the past.

Henry Anatole Grunwald, a senior editor of Time, *writes frequently for* HORIZON. *His introduction to* Salinger: A Critical Portrait, *which he edited, appeared in the May, 1962, issue.*

At Home Through the Ages

Drawings by PHILIPPE JULIAN

In the opinion of the French satirist Philippe Julian a chair should never be mistaken as primarily a thing to sit on. An empty chair, properly considered, is a negative print of a personality. When the person comes to occupy it, the chair will be complete. In the same way a drawing room or a decorative style is not a room or even a collection of furniture: it is a personality. A Victorian drawing room, to take an obvious example, evokes Queen Victoria; the Hall of Mirrors at Versailles is complete only in the presence of *le Roi Soleil*. (Just so, your living room is, for better or for worse, you.) There are, however, key figures in the history of interior decoration who are not so well recognized. Some of them are even fictional, but they have been influential, nevertheless. In a collection published recently in Paris, *Les Styles*, Philippe Julian identifies them; a selection from his book follows.

The domination of décor by personality began early. Here is Nero, flanked by a bust of an ancestor, calling on his mother, Agrippina. Ancestors, as Agrippina was to learn, were expendable; their busts, however, were indispensable to classical style.

What finer occupation for an eccentric English gentleman of the late eighteenth century than the drafting of his family tree? Sir William Beckford, early prophet of the Gothic revival, is here seen ensconced in his famous Fonthill Abbey, the greatest of his "restorations."

Goethe and his faithful Eckermann made of Weimar a new Athens, but it was a gemütlich Athens: the lyres, swans, and pillars were a little squat, the chairs always comfortable. Biedermeier, as the style came to be called, took root ineradicably in royal apartments from Copenhagen to Vienna.

Madame Bovary, playing her inlaid piano in the provinces, was as pure a cultural force as any real lady. For her the industrial revolution opened a whole new world: imitation Cellinis, Raphaels in lithograph, and a peculiar style of tufted upholstery soon to capture the bourgeoisie everywhere.

The magnitude of Rothschild finance was matched only by the grand sweep of Rothschild décor. Its aim, simple in its purity, was to gather as much stuff as possible in one place—from Fragonards and Genoese velvets to Savonneries and snuffboxes. Highly durable, it flourishes today from Dallas to Newport, wherever ostentation is admired.

The Poet in a Valley of Dry

Granted a genuine sense of vocation, what technical advice can a young poet be offered? I dislike the word "technique." One hears: "Yes, he (or she) doesn't *move* me in the least, but ah! what dazzling technique!" This implies intellectual achievement in any near-magical art or craft from which the intellect should, I believe, be barred for truth's sake, except as an occasional consultant on simple fact. Very well, then: What advice on craftsmanship, even if craftsmanship now means something quaint, laborious, and out-of-date? But advice is what everybody gives and nobody takes.

As a young poet, I wrote my first serious poem in the summer of 1906, when I was eleven years old. I had been turned out of the family wagonette by my short-tempered grandfather, for having climbed aboard without my school cap, and so missed a picnic beside the river. I spent the afternoon working out a country poem in rhymed couplets about a farmer who, so far as I recall, prudently harvested and carted his wheat just before a hailstorm flattened the crops of all his less industrious neighbors. The poem ended with this couplet:

> *The swain gave thanks at daybreak for God's grace;*
> *At Kirk this morn I saw his smiling face.*

I remember thinking that *swain* and *kirk* and *morn* were very elegant words, and that I had scored off my grandfather (to whom, on his return, I dedicated the poem) by showing how little I cared for family picnics. This was a false start. Three years later I felt a genuine afflatus, and wrote one moonlit night in June:

> *O, not for me the lute or lyre!*
> *A knight, I ride my thoughts of fire*
> *And fly on wings for ever and aye*
> *Through an unresisting starry sky.*
> *Where the gleaming aether turns and sings*
> *Its strange slow song of the birth of things.*

There was a difference in kind between these two failures: the first, an academic exercise, was sadly deficient in technique; the second, a personal statement, was equally deficient in craftsmanship—but my hand trembled as I wrote it down; nor did I parade it for public approval.

One often meets a musical prodigy, but never a poetic prodigy, of tender age. A long, long experience with language is needed before words can fully collaborate with one another under the poetic trance. It seems necessary, too, to have read a great many poems by other writers, good and bad, before a poet can realize his powers and limitations. I never have much use for one whose poems I do not recognize at a glance as inimitably his own; even so, I reject them if they draw attention to a cultivated eccentricity, to pride in scholarship, or to mastery of Classical or Modernist technique.

Shakespeare's plays can be arranged in chronological order, and the development of his verse-craftsmanship studied; but I am not a playgoer, and the comparatively rare occasions when he included poems in his theatrical declamations are all that really interest me. Some plays contain no more than a couple of lines; in others there are scenes consisting of poem sequences strung together on a thread of dramatic dialogue. Popular conventions were as strong in Shakespeare's day as now, and he could not afford to disregard them. No poet ever escapes from the epoch into which he is born; he can only transcend conventions by showing where they do not apply to him. And he should have a sense of belonging to a long line of former free spirits, and decide whether their divergences from contemporary fashion merit his approval; Shakespeare, despite his limited schooling, seems to have been fantastically well-read.

The history of English poetry is traced in the text books as a succession of movements or schools—the School of Chaucer, the Allegorical School, the early Tudor Drama-

Bones

By ROBERT GRAVES

xact right word, and it sometimes takes a poet his lifetime to find it—if he ever does

tists, the Euphuists, and so on, past the Anti-Jacobins, the Lake School, the mid-Victorian Romantics, etc., until one reaches the Georgians, the Imagists, and the Modernist Movement. But schools and movements are fictions. If a school, meaning the disciples and imitators of a particular verse-craftsman, achieves fashionable renown, this is a grave criticism of his sincerity: a poet should be inimitable. When two genuine poets recognize each other as true to their common vocation, this will only accentuate the difference between them in rhythm, diction, and the rest. Any talk of a "school" means that someone is peddling a new technique of verbal conjuring, as in commercial schools that teach writers of advertising copy how to make easily hypnotizable subjects buy what they themselves could not possibly believe in.

Craftsmanship is self-taught. A poet lives with his own language, continually instructing himself in the origin, histories, pronunciation, and peculiar usages of words, together with their latent powers and the exact shades of distinction between what *Roget's Thesaurus* calls "synonyms" —but are there such things? English has no officially approved way of expressing every conceivable thought, as French has; only precedents. A poet may make his own precedents, in disregard of any law of correctness laid down by grammarians—so long as they accord with the natural genius of English. I studied French, Latin, Greek, grammar at school, back in the reign of King Edward the Peacemaker, but was told: "Only foreign languages have grammar," and expected to be treated as an imbecile or a yokel if I spoke or wrote bad English. Its proper use was held to be a matter of good manners, not of grammatic law: I still hold this to be so.

Only wide reading, a retentive ear for conversation, and continuous dwelling upon words as disembodied spirits rather than as building materials, can equip a poet for his task. And what does "equip" mean? It comes from the medieval Latin *eschipare,* "to man a ship," but had be-

come metaphorical even before reaching England—Cardinal Wolsey uses it, first, in the sense of finding soldiers the necessary arms and accoutrements for battle. The poet should be aware, however, that the word *ship* is still latent in *equip,* and therefore so is the sense of making ready for a voyage.

In a true poem, produced by the deep trance that integrates all the memories of the mind, the dormant powers of each word awake and combine with those of every other, building up a tremendous head of power. How far the reader is conscious of the interrelated sounds and meanings depends on how much of a poet he, or she, is: for I allow the title of poet to all who think poetically, whether they are writers or not.

A historical dictionary should always be within a poet's reach—preferably the big *Oxford English Dictionary* (the two-volume edition is insufficient). More than thirty years ago, when I could not afford a set, I remembered the New Testament parable of the pearl, sold all my nonessential books, and bought it. I still consult the O.E.D. at least four or five times a day, never letting a doubtful word go by; I need to know its derivation, its first occurrence, its change of meaning down the centuries, and the sort of people who used it in different contexts.

The Vienna school of psychology presumes a conscious and unconscious mind as two separate and usually warring entities; but a poet cannot accept this. In the poetic trance, he has access not only to the primitive emotions and thoughts that lie stored in his childhood memory, but to all his subsequent experiences—emotional and intellectual—including a wide knowledge of English won by constant critical study. Words are filed away by the hundred thousand, not in alphabetic order but in related groups; and as soon as the trance seizes him, he can single out most of the ones he needs. Moreover, when the first heavily blotted draft has been copied out afresh the

85

last thing at night, and laid aside for reconsideration, he will read it the next morning as if it were written by another hand. Yet soon he is back in the trance, finds that while he was asleep his mind has been active on another problem, and that he can substitute the exact right word for the stand-in with which he had to be content the night before.

One cannot hope to restore the creative processes that supplied certain unusual words in ancient poems. The work sheets very rarely survive as evidence, and to discuss my own experience in writing poems suggests that I claim poetic merit for them, which no poet can afford to do. All poems are failures in the Muse's eye; and it is this conviction alone that entitles me to discuss the weaknesses in the work of others. One of the Muse's main functions is to abash her poet by making him aware of his stupidities, vanities, and petty dishonesties.

I once wrote a poem called "A Time of Waiting," the theme of which was a resolve not to prejudice the future by hasty action:

> *To take no rash decisions, enter into*
> *No random friendships, check the run-away tongue*
> *And fix my mind in a close pattern of doubt . . .*

When reviewing the second or third draft, I saw that *pattern* was too decorative a word.

> *And fix my mind in a close* frame *of doubt . . .*

would have been too formal. I tried:

> *And fix my mind in a close* net *of doubt . . .*

But a mind can hardly be fixed in a net; besides, *net* has the negative connotation of imprisonment without escape. I had in mind a positive form of quiet doubt, cultivated for the sake of good luck, because the Muse, for whose sake the doubt was assumed, would clearly not hasten to remove it. Finding the exact word seemed of the greatest importance: the poem, when complete, would confirm me in my decision. Poems have an autohypnotic function.

When I am writing prose and have a word on the tip of my tongue, or the nib of my pen, which somehow eludes me, I often consult *Roget's Thesaurus.* Reading the list of so-called synonyms in a word group, I at once recognize the word I need. But I do not use *Roget* for poems. So, instead, on this occasion I went down to the sea, swam out to a small rocky island, and there the exact right word floated up to me from several fathoms down:

> *To take no rash decisions, enter into*
> *No random friendships, check the run-away tongue*
> *And fix my mind in a close caul of doubt.*

Caul surprised me, because I had not used or considered it for at least twenty years; but, reaching for the "C" vol-

ume of the O.E.D., I found that the word held all the meanings I needed. A caul is, first, a net cap confining the glory of a woman, her hair; then, a gossamer web spun by spiders over grass, heavy with dew at dawn; finally, it is the smooth, caplike membrane with which a child is sometimes born, a lucky relic of his uterine experiences and, in English superstition, sovereign against death by drowning. A caul is thus the gentlest and happiest of all cerebral restraints. I found three metaphorical uses of *caul,* which set a precedent for mine:

1579—*Whoso is blinded with the caul of beauty . . .*
1636—*Custom in sin has drawn a caul over my conscience.*
1643—*A caul drawn on the heart.*

That *close call* has a somewhat outmoded slang significance was an accident that did not disturb me. The eye cannot mistake *caul* for *call,* and the eye commands the inner ear. Poetry is read, not listened to, nine times out of ten. And *close* was the right adjective to qualify *caul;* I would have been ungrateful to look for another.

If a poem is lurking at the back of a poet's mind, and he has perfect confidence in bringing it to light under the trance, the key words sooner or later will always fall into place. Or that is my own long-cherished superstition.

On the sole occasion that I ever discussed poetry with Walter de la Mare, I quoted him the lines from his "All That's Past":

> *—Oh, no man knows*
> *Through what wild centuries*
> *Roves back the rose . . .*

and asked whether he was satisfied with *roves.* He blushed slightly, and admitted that though *roves* was too close in sound to *rose,* it was the nearest he could get—no, he wasn't satisfied. He needed some word that had the sense of *rambling,* as roses ramble; he had tried *Twines back the rose,* but *wild* and *twines* made an ugly assonance:

> *Through what wild centuries*
> *Twines back the rose . . .*

Gads back the rose had a precedent in Milton's *gadding vine,* but *gad* was too similar in sound to *back* and, since Milton's days, had acquired a vulgar sense from *gadabout.*

De la Mare died without finding a satisfactory solution to the problem, perhaps because he was dealing with a conceit, not a poetic thought; and because the technical trick of metathesis—transferring the adjective *wild* from *rose* to *centuries*—had thrown the stanza out of gear. I have no hope of finding the exact right answer myself, because it was never my poem. I have tried ineffectually:

> *—Oh, no man knows*
> *From what lost centuries*
> *Wanders the rose . . .*

and I have also tried:

> *What old, dead centuries*
> *Bred the wild rose . . .*

But if it has to be *wild centuries,* then:

> *Through what wild centuries*
> *Wends back the rose . . .*

is certainly better than *roves back. Wend,* a De-la-Mareish word, is akin to *wander* and *winding,* and makes a nice alliteration with *wild.*

The exact right word is sometimes missing from the dictionary. Thomas Hardy told me, in 1924 or so, that he now made it his practice to confirm doubtful words and that, a few days before, when looking up one such in the *Oxford English Dictionary,* he had found it, to be sure. But the only reference was: "Thomas Hardy: *Far From the Madding Crowd,* 1874."

I have myself hoped to contribute two or three words to the language. In a satire, "Beauty in Trouble," I had occasion to mention the batlike wings and cloven hooves of an evil angel. But *batlike* is a plain, guileless, Anglo-Saxon word, and the context demanded a rather grandiloquent Romance one to barb the satire. *Catlike* and *feline; doglike* and *canine; horselike* and *equine;* these pairs, although synonyms to *Roget,* lie worlds apart. One sees the difference best in the phrase "doglike devotion." "Canine devotion" is not stubborn personal love but mere animal behaviorism. Very well: *batlike* needs an equivalent formed from the Latin—as *feline* is from *felis, canine* from *canis, equine* from *equus.* The Latin for *bat* is *vespertilio;* so I coined the word *vespertilian—vespertilionian* seemed too much of a mouthful:

> *The fiend who beats, betrays and sponges on her,*
> *Persuades her, white is black,*
> *Flaunts vespertilian wing and cloven hoof*
> *And soon will fetch her back . . .*

Among the gaps in the *Oxford English Dictionary* is *garden:* a jeweler's term for the bright cloudiness in certain gems, caused by chemical impurities but giving them individuality and character. I am told that such a *garden* now proves that a stone is genuine: the chemists who can artificially produce genuine rubies, emeralds, sapphires, and the rest have not yet got round to making any but flawlessly translucent ones:

> *The pale rose-amethyst on her breast*
> *Has such a garden in it*
> *Your eye could wander there for hours*
> *And wonder and be lost.*

Last year I addressed the American Academy of Arts and Letters on the Arabic word *báraka,* which means the lively virtue, or blessedness, that a place or object acquires by long use; and deplored the new economic doctrine of built-in obsolescence, which sweeps out-of-date models into the junk yard or the garbage can long before they are worn out and replaces them with others not meant to last for more than a short season. The lively virtue in words is longer lasting. The doctrine of expendability applies either to semi-scientific terms, which go out of date as the theses on which they rest are disproved, or to slang coinages of novel terms for words like *money, liquor, girl, steal, cheat, policeman, fornicate, get drunk, die,* which add nothing to the simple original concept. A policeman is neither less nor more of a policeman when he is called a peeler, a bobby, an ecilop, a slop, a cop, a copper, a rozzer, a bull, or a fuzz. Slang has been called "poor man's poetry," perhaps because eighteenth-century Classical tradition insisted on a particularized poetic vocabulary; and so did the Romantic Revivalists, though preferring a "Gothic" range of words borrowed from Chaucer, Spenser, Shakespeare, Walpole, and Chatterton. Walter de la Mare is said to have started as a poet by compiling lists of mellifluous words, such as *bergamot, chrysoprase, cresset, foredone, besprent,* and introducing them into nostalgic rhymes: his was a deliberate technique of quaintness.

The longer a word lasts in a language before growing obsolete—and one of a poet's moral duties is to rescue and reinstate obsolescent words for which no substitute can be found—the more strength and virtue it acquires. Yet there are well-dressed poems as well as naked ones, and the choice of vocabulary must always be directed by the theme. Donne, for example, specializes in the costumed poem, rather than the naked one. His "Seventh Elegy" alternates between the two different strands of language, Anglo-Saxon and Norman-French, rather than integrating them:

> Nature's lay Ideot, *I taught thee to love,*
> And in that sophistrie, Oh, thou dost prove
> Too subtile: *Foole, thou didst not understand*
> The mystique language *of the eye nor hand:*
> *Nor couldst thou judge* the difference of the aire
> *Of sighes, and say, this lies,* this sounds despaire . . .

He is working up to the grand close of five splendid Romance words, introduced with eight Anglo-Saxon ones:

> *I had not taught thee then the* Alphabet
> Of flowers, how they devisefully *being set*
> *And bound up, might with speechless* secrecie
> Deliver arrands mutely, *and* mutually.

Donne gets away with a portentous word, *interinanimate,* in "The Ecstasie," by using only Anglo-Saxon words to introduce it:

> *When love with one another so*
> *Interinanimates two souls . . .*

Shakespeare gets away in *Macbeth* with:

> *. . . This my hand will rather*
> *The multitudinous seas incarnadine . . .*

these being terrifying words suited to Lady Macbeth's guilt and redeemed from bombast by the even more terrifying simplicity of the Anglo-Saxon line that follows:

> *Making the green one red . . .*

To *incarnadine* and *to make red* are not, as is usually thought, tautological; and though *incarnadine* meant only *make carnation-colored,* like healthy cheeks, Shakespeare was aware of its ultimate origin in the Latin *caro, carnis*— "flesh"—and therefore of its association with words like *carnifex* and *carnivorous.* He so aroused the latent meaning of murder in *incarnadine* that one cannot use it today without thinking of blood.

The lively virtue of words is something of which every poet must be aware. *England* has this virtue, and so has *Scotland*; but not *Britain,* which is an intellectual, not an emotional, concept. Nor has *Britons* much virtue, despite:

> *Rule, Britannia! Britannia, rule the waves!*
> *Britons never, never, never shall be slaves . . .*

The adjective *British,* curiously enough, *has* acquired virtue because of the British Fleet, the British Grenadiers, and so on.

The exact rightness of words can be explained only in the context of a whole poem, each one being related rhythmically, emotionally, and semantically to every other. This, in effect, rules out any use of the same word in different contexts, unless the two uses are consonant, or parallel. It also rules out any repetition of the same vowel sound, unless for some particular purpose, such as the deliberate stridency of repeated long *a* and *i*. Or as when Keats, who insisted on the need to vary vowel sounds in ordinary contexts, commends Shakespeare for writing of the bees:

> *The singing masons building roofs of gold . . .*

The four short *i*-sounds in *singing* and *building,* he said, suggested the low buzz of bees.

A poem always chooses its own meter, and any attempt to dress up an idea in a particular meter is, at best, an amusing parlor game; at worst, dreary literature. A poem begins with the usual line-and-a-half that unexpectedly forces itself on the entranced mind and establishes not only the meter, but its rhythmic treatment. The basic English meter is the ten-syllabled iambic line, but the metrical rules—which in Latin poetry were always meticulously maintained, even though the context might be a passionate one—do not apply to English. A true iambic line in poems of emotional content has been rare since early Tudor times, and appears usually in lulls be-

tween gusts. The Earl of Surrey's proud requiem for his friend and companion-in-arms Thomas Clere begins not in the measured iambic style but with a drum beat,

> *Norfolk sprung thee; Lambeth holds thee dead.*
> *Clere of the Count of Cleremont thou hight . . .*

before the iambic measure asserts itself:

> *Within the womb of Ormond's race thou bred*
> *And saw'st thy cousin crownèd in thy sight . . .*

Shakespeare, in his indignant sonnet,

> *Were't aught to me I bore the canopy,*
> *With my extern the outward honouring . . .*

does much the same thing. The rhythmic variations on this iambic line are infinite; yet, at the back of the mind, the meter still reigns.

The choice made by Modernists of the 1920's to dispense with meter and rhyme altogether, because their Classically-minded predecessors had let these direct the poem, was unnecessary. Granted, a poet whose gentle voice rises and falls regularly in the iambic meter, with the expected rhyme closing each line, cannot hold my attention long. But whoever relies on what he calls "cadence," as opposed to variations in meter, or changes the norm constantly without warning, cannot expect the Muse to approve or the reader to follow him.

A young poet finds his greatest difficulty in ending a poem. The sudden occurrence of a poetic phrase and an idea is not enough: unless he recognizes that a complete poem is there, let him be patient. He has perhaps not yet learned how to integrate his whole mind in the necessary trance of attention. Donne is an extreme example of impatience: he often begins with splendid candor and ends in crooked artifice.

When one treats poetry in this way, the notion of technique falls away: all that remains is the poet's service to the Muse, his unwavering love of whom, for all her unpossessability, assures that his work will be truthful. Every dictionary is a valley of dry bones. The poet is inspired to breathe life into them (as Ezekiel did when he prophesied) and convert them into language. You remember the rattle and shaking, and how the bones came together into skeletons, every bone to its bone, and put on sinews and flesh. That is a metaphor of craftsmanship. Then the four winds blew upon them, and they stood up, in fighting companies —which is how poems come alive. Technique takes one no farther than articulating the skeletons with wire, and plumping them up with plastic limbs and organs.

One of England's leading men of letters, Robert Graves was in 1961 elected Professor of Poetry in Oxford University, an honor that calls upon him to deliver an annual series of lectures. This text is adapted from one of the most recent.

BOWLING GOES BOURGEOIS

By RUSSELL LYNES

Once the haunts of toughs and drifters, the ten-pin alleys now are seeking to capture the wholesome, middle-class trade, and are decorated accordingly

In Great Barrington, Massachusetts, where I frequently spend Saturday evening in one of the local bowling alleys called Bowlero (twenty years ago such a statement would have sounded like an admission of depravity), I commented to a lady with whom I was bowling (and she most certainly was a lady) that it was rather odd, wasn't it, that this emporium of athletic prowess and all-American fun should be painted in turquoise and orchid?

"Good heavens," the lady said, looking up from the score sheet, "so it is. I never noticed."

What has happened to the bowling alley is in short a phenomenon—undeniable in its vastness, gaudy in its effects, and perhaps a little bit confusing in its significance. As an institution, the bowling alley used to show more than a trace of the unwholesome; it was commonly joined with a poolroom as well, and was a hangout for bookies and con men of various seedy sorts. Now all this has changed; bowling has become a family sport, unabashedly clean and clean-cut, with manners and customs—and décor—to match.

A bowling alley is, of course, essentially a one-purpose gymnasium, but what has happened is that some elements of the Turkish bath have crept into it. It is now a multipurpose palace of rejuvenation, a fillip to eye and spirit and whatever other appetites its designers and proprietors can decently encompass

—and decency is *de rigueur*. The bowling alley manages to maintain it while at the same time suggesting a certain amount of mystery, sensuality, and just plain honky-tonk. It is in many ways the 1960's counterpart of the movie palace of the 1920's. It is as though one had squeezed Roxy's or Grauman's Chinese in Hollywood or the old Oriental Loew's Seventy-second Street through the Bauhaus and come out with the gilt and fake stars and arabesques smoothed flat but none the less gaudy—a long, low palace that outside looks like Edward D. Stone piled on Edward D. Stone and inside like an enormous pin-ball machine.

Several weeks ago I spent an evening in the most elaborate of all such contraptions (they seem more like gadgets than like architecture) in Willow Grove, Pennsylvania, a suburb of Philadelphia. All I knew about it before I went there was that it was "the biggest bowling alley" in the world, that it had been described by its proprietor as "all-out modern," and that it had under one roof *one hundred and sixteen* alleys! (This is the sort of statement that makes bowlers whistle with disbelief; non-

bowlers are unimpressed. To bowling enthusiasts who think that a row of thirty alleys is pretty impressive and sixty is miraculous, it is like saying that there is a county in Pennsylvania entirely occupied by one bowling establishment; like the outer-space chatter of children it makes no sense.)

The name of this establishment is the Willow Grove Park Lanes, and it bills itself as "The Bowling Palace of the World." In addition to one hundred and sixteen bowling alleys, it has three restaurants, a nursery where mothers can leave their littlest children while they bowl (any but the littlest children today bowl themselves), two recreation areas filled with pinball machines and snooker tables, a place for full-sized billiard and pool tables, a "pro" shop full of bowling balls and bowling shoes, and ball bags and shoe bags, and socks and Band-Aids, and other equipment for the bowlers. It has been open only since last August, and it is the very latest word in bowling and may possibly continue to be so for five minutes more; things move terribly fast in the bowling world (though a slight grinding noise has recently been heard) and what is up-to-date today can seem primitive tomorrow.

At the Willow Grove Park Lanes one can see the new shapes and styles of bowling blossom in full flower. The establishment's aesthetics (if I may use the word in this connection) cost two and a half million dollars (another million and a half went into automatic pin-setting machines and the gleaming maple alleys), and belong in that family of flat-chested but muscular rococo to which a great many motels and shopping centers also belong. Richness is achieved by using a great variety of materials for the exterior and (since that doesn't seem to be enough) by floodlighting it with lights that change color or, at least, cast different hues on different parts of the building. Wil-

"A bowling alley is, of course, essentially a

low Grove, for example (the building is essentially a very shallow V with fifty-eight alleys in each of the wings), uses on its outside highly glazed and bright blue brick, a pierced wall in the Edward D. Stone convention (or, more properly, cliché), fieldstone of almost boulder proportions, colored concrete, a gravel wall (large smooth pebbles), and wood that sticks out in fins slightly reminiscent of the way Frank Lloyd Wright used them years ago at Taliesin West. This is further elaborated with free-form green gardens, reflecting pools, fountains with changing lights, and even at one point gas flames that shoot out of a wall over water to make an effect that sounds spectacular but was busted the evening I was there. Puncinello's nose, from the classic Neopolitan masques, sticks out over the main entrance supported, the manager told me, by the biggest beam that Bethlehem Steel has ever made. It is sky-blue on the outside and ecru on the underside.

Indoors the decoration manages to combine the quaint, the exotic, the utilitarian, the gay, and the monumental in order to provide something for every taste, and a great deal for people with no taste at all. One of the three restaurants is called the Hofbrau ("He-Man Sandwiches—Imported Beer") in which the tables are oak-stained barrels with round table tops set on them and the seats are kegs with round red cushions on their tops. Another restaurant, the Waterfall Room ("Dine to the soothing play of cascading water"), situated on several levels, has a bar behind which are set, in a dark wall, circles of multicolored luminescent mosaic from Italy (and lighted with a purple light that makes them glow), and a waterfall that can be turned on and off with a switch and spills five hundred gallons of water a minute over shelves of stone into a pool. It sounded to me a little like a hydrant turned loose in a city street. "We never keep it on for very long at a time," Stanley Raytinsky, the

manager of the establishment, told me. "Some people find it a little tiring."

The operative part of Willow Grove Park Lanes is, of course, the alleys themselves. If you allow roughly six feet for the width of an alley and its gutters and another foot for the ball-return for each pair of alleys, you will find that one hundred and sixteen alleys would make a width of about 760 feet. If you add to this the space that is allowed at Willow Grove for the billiard and pool tables and the pro shop between the two sets of fifty-eight alleys, you will discover that the roof of this building is roughly three times the length of a football field. This ceiling, where it covers the alleys, is white acoustical tile and curves down in a saw-toothed fashion, from the high space above the players to the pins, in such a way that the ceiling throws the noise of flying pins back upon itself. (The Willow Grove Lanes are quieter than the Bowlero, which has only twelve alleys.) Considering the number of ten- to sixteen-pound balls that are thrown onto hard wood and the number of pins made of wood coated with plastic that they scatter, modern bowling alleys are extraordinarily quiet.

In all modern alleys the pins are set by machine, and in the

one-purpose gymnasium"

newest alleys there is a triangle above the pins that lights up after the first ball in each turn is thrown and indicates which pins are left standing. If a strike is made (that is, all ten pins are knocked down by the first ball), a sort of crown (the emblem of the Brunswick Corporation, one of three companies that makes pin-setting machines) lights up in red. In other words the bowling alley has in fact become a great deal more like the standard saloon or ice-cream-parlor pinball game (you throw a ball, there is a fine rumble and crash, and lights flash on) than it used to be in the past when the pins were set by what were euphemistically called "boys." There is a refinement at Willow Grove, however, that I have not seen elsewhere. Each pair of alleys leads up to what could easily be (above the pins and the indicator showing which pins are standing) the white-and-gold-trimmed headboard of a noble double bed, designed, of course, for a royal couple. Otherwise why the crown in its center? Otherwise why should the crown turn red when perfection is achieved?

The Willow Grove Lanes may be the biggest bowling alley in the world, but it is not the fanciest; it is only one of about ten thousand bowling centers in the United States and its alleys are a drop in a bucket, numerous as they are. There are 148,535 alleys in America, or were in August, 1962, when the American Bowling Congress and the Bowling Proprietors' Association of America, the two major bowling associations, reported their strength. Each alley costs $4,500 to build, and each automatic pin-setting machine costs "about $8,500" whether it is built by Brunswick or by American Machine and Foundry, which produced the first practicable machine in 1952 and revolutionized the bowling industry. There are estimated to be about twenty-four million Americans who are fairly regular bowlers, and the bowling business runs to "an estimated" one and a half billion dollars a year. This glut of money and people should give you some idea of the limits to which people will go to take out their aggressions amiably and in the presence of their friends.

Bowling is an ancient sport in America, but if it has become wholesome, it has not become chic or fashionable, and it is not

92

likely to. It was the Dutch who introduced bowling to America in the seventeenth century. Gamblers were delighted with it but the community fathers were not, and it was outlawed. Someone, however, noticed that only "nine pins" were banned and introduced the game of ten pins set in a triangle, which is the game played today. (William Longgood in the New York *World-Telegram* recently said: "The Puritans took no action against the revised version. One wit observed, 'It opened up the 7-10 split, and that was penance enough.'" If you do not understand this joke, you are not a bowler and never have been one.)

Until 1952, when the automatic pin setters were introduced, there were "boys" in the pit to collect the pins as they were knocked down and to return the balls. Pin boys were not usually the most stable members of society. Many of them set pins to get enough money for a "fix" or a drink; they floated from one alley to another; they were sometimes aged and slow and infirm; they sometimes insulted women who bowled (ladies never bowled much in those days) by putting mash notes in the finger holes of the balls before returning them. But they were by no means all of that sort. Many of them set pins in the winter and worked as stable boys at the tracks in summer. Some of them had regular jobs, which they supplemented by setting pins; a few managed to make enough money to buy themselves a higher education. But whoever they were, they were an element in the game that had a kind of friendly charm and humanity now missing.

In the 1940's and early 1950's I used to take my children (illegally—by New York City law minors were not allowed in bowling alleys that served liquor) to an establishment in the west nineties on Sunday afternoons. The proprietor evidently slipped the cop on the beat a fin to look the other way; we were not the only family there. We got to know several of the pin boys (this was an alley of eight lanes), and they knew how we bowled. When one of the children made a strike (or almost made one) or a spare or managed to convert a split, the pin boy might very well clap. Occasionally when there were just two pins left standing the boy would put another pin on top of each to make two splendid steeples; the children loved it. Once in a while I would see the pin boy gently nudge a pin with his toe and make it fall down if he thought that a ball was well-thrown by one of the children but wasn't quite good enough to make the spare. Unfortunately this minor and harmless kind of chicanery is now gone. An automatic pin setter can get out of order, but it cannot encourage a ten-year-old or make him laugh or cheat just a tiny bit in his favor.

In fact this is precisely the sort of thing that people in the bowling business (or should it more properly be called "industry?") have been trying to get rid of. The association of the bowling alley with its location over a saloon on Railroad Street, reached by dusty creaking stairs and inhabited by the town bums, clung to the sport until after the Second World War. Bowling was "vulgar" and one didn't find "nice" people engaged in it. Actually the sport has been growing in popularity and respectability for about thirty years. Women began to bowl in the 1930's and, according to Pat McDonough of the *World-Telegram*, "When they first appeared in the Glenwood Manor alley in Queens . . . the management shielded them with a curtain around the lanes they used."

Recently there has been a conscientious effort on the part of bowling impresarios to make the language of bowling more genteel. The unfortunate connotations of "bowling alleys" is met with insistence that the establishments drop the word *alleys* and substitute *lanes*. But there is another refinement that seems downright nineteenth-century in its attempt at gentility. The word "gutters," as the troughs down either side of a "lane" have always been called, are now spoken of as "channels."

In general the great increase in the popularity of bowling in recent years is ascribed by those in the industry to the automation of the alleys (pin setters), the fact that women have found it to be a form of recreation they enjoy, and third, the promotion the sport has received from television programs. To these should also be added two obvious other reasons for the bowling boom: increased leisure time and money in people's pockets. But, bowling proprietors are dissatisfied with the rate at which business expands and have resorted to elaborate gimmicks to make it more attractive to housewives, especially, and to youngsters. The baby-sitting function (so elaborately tended to at Willow Grove with mock-up trains and ships and even a whale for the tots to toddle in) has become more or less standard in suburban bowling emporiums. A good many alleys have laundry machines so that their female customers can get their wash done while they bowl. One establishment in Burbank, California, supplements its twenty-four lanes with "a swimming pool, billiard room, riding stable, two restaurants, and a ballroom." The manager explains: "We want to have something that every member of the family can do." An alley in suburban Chicago is reported to have "a full-time sociologist to integrate the center with the community."

The backbone of the bowling industry is by no means the casual bowling family that drops in of an evening (some families are willing, however, to wait more than two hours to get an alley; most alleys do not take private reservations). The big business is in the leagues—thousands upon thousands of them in industries, churches, stores, country clubs. They are made up of teams that bowl regularly one night a week. They always bowl three games (at fifty cents a game) and are very likely to consume a profitable amount of beer while doing so. It is almost impossible to get a lane in any alley in America on any weekday

"Now a multipurpose palace of rejuvenation . . ."

evening between six o'clock and ten. The alleys then are entirely occupied by league teams, often clad in silk shirts of intense colors with the name of the team in elaborate script on the back and the bowler's first name or nickname over the breast pocket. The manager at Willow Grove, a great deal of whose time goes into persuading groups in his community to form leagues, said that in four hours on any evening he could handle 1,152 teams in two shifts. He would be delighted (as any bowling proprietor would be) to have a great many more afternoon leagues.

Bowling is a militantly lower-middlebrow sport and thoroughly Non-U, and in spite of efforts to alter its social complexion (which, let it be said, is its principal strength) it will continue to be so. The American Machine & Foundry Company (AMF), in an effort to make bowling at least look a little more chic than it normally does, has encouraged a number of European dress designers to create fashions especially for bowlers, and last July at the Syosset (Long Island) Lanes the company presented a collection of "skirts, pants, culottes, shirts, jackets, and sweaters." The designs came from couturiers as distinguished as Chanel of Paris and Fabiani and the Princess Galitzine of Rome, but lest AMF (whose foreign business is considerable) seem to play national favorites, there were also designs from Mexico City, Dublin, London, Munich, and Florence. It seems likely that AMF is the only manufacturer of heavy machinery now in the ladies' fashion business. A good many department stores, in addition, now advertise bowling costumes. The makers of "Permalift" produce something called an "Adorabowl panty," which is "packaged in a replica of a bowling ball"

and which, of course, "won't ride up." In the most recent AMF equipment catalogue, called "New Fashion Line of Bowling Balls, Bags and Shoes," the Italian influence is especially strong in shoes for both men and women; they are long and multicolored and pointed. Brunswick, not to be outdone, sells bowling shoes designed by Capezio of ballet-slipper fame. Bowling balls, which used to be a standard black or Venetian red or occasionally marbleized in rather retiring colors (dark green on black, for instance) now come in colors as bright as all-day suckers. AMF makes one called the "Holiday Ball" that is a marbleized mixture of all the colors in an oil slick on a background of pearl-gray. Brunswick offers "cornflower-blue" and "explosive-pink" balls for the ladies.

The reasons why bowling will never be fashionable but will continue to be popular are built into the structures that house it, into its economics, and into the nature of the sport itself. The buildings, whatever they may derive from in the various vocabularies of contemporary architecture, all have one quality in common: they are palaces for the people in precisely the same way that the Mississippi river boat, with its gilt-and-white Gothic tracery, its expanses of flowered Brussels carpet, and its silver samovars, was a public palace. The luxury of the ships may sometimes have been tawdry but, as Mark Twain said, "they tallied with the citizen's dream of what magnificence was, and satisfied it."

This kind of magnificence is available to everyone in a bowling alley at the same price. The standard charge for bowling is fifty cents a game (or "string" or "line"), and though some alleys charge a little less in the afternoon, or for children under

"A fillip to eye and spirit, and other appetites"

sixteen, or in the summer when bowling suffers from competition with outdoor sports, the price is the same in the most magnificent and in the most commonplace establishments. There is, in other words, no way that a bowler by paying more money can go to an "exclusive" alley and thus upstage other bowlers, and by the same token there is no way for him to make bowling into a class game. One can, by contrast, sit in a box at a baseball game and be exclusive; there is no way to be exclusive in a bowling alley. The economics of the game make it impossible.

The game itself is also a leveler in a rather remarkable and reverse way that is not true of any other sport I can think of. In bowling it is quite possible to make a very high score just because the winds of fortune are blowing your way. A bowler who averages 130 a game will, if he bowls fairly regularly, every now and then make a score above 200 or even, though rarely, above 230. These are the kinds of scores he sees the professionals make on television, and, of course, he immediately becomes one of them in his own estimation. He thinks of himself as a "potential 200 bowler." "If only," he says under his breath, "I could do this all the time and really practice, I'd. . . ." Such a situation never obtains in golf. Does a duffer who plays around 100 ever shoot a game in the seventies? In bowling an occasional high score tends to create the illusion that all bowlers are one.

The bowling industry has recently run into trouble; it has overbuilt. In an increasing number of communities there are more alleys than can be operated profitably. The tendency has been to build fancier and fancier establishments—richer and richer, and more and more like palaces—to tempt customers away from the competition. "The big bowling boom everyone has been talking about," said the director of the Dallas-Fort Worth Bowling Proprietors' Association to a *Wall Street Journal* reporter in March, 1962, "is a boom in construction, not in new bowlers. We've about reached the saturation point right now." There was an unpleasant tremor in the industry last spring that seemed to bear this out. The Department of Justice filed an anti-trust suit against "the operators of bowling centers and the manufacturers of bowling equipment." The Government charged that they had "sought to prevent competition by restricting the construction of new centers and the expansion of existing ones." The matter is still being argued, but the symptoms of overgrowth are painful, however the courts may find.

Overgrowth, which is at least partly the result of a battle of plush-and-plenty against public indifference, may cause the proprietors anxiety but it can delight the bowlers. Even in Great Barrington the Bowlero has suffered from competition with a larger, gaudier, more palatial institution called The Cove just a few miles away. More lights flash on at The Cove when the ball strikes the pins; there are vaster areas of carpeting, the wall ornaments are fancier, the noises more subdued. The battle for patronage is being waged with the aesthetics of honky-tonk and the midway only slightly toned down, with the colored moving lights of the jukebox and the pinball machine. It is the story of the river boats and "opry" houses and movie palaces all over again. For all its palatial pretentiousness the bowling alley has an undeniable, inflexible, and somewhat unforgivable tone of good clean American respectability.

Russell Lynes, author of The Tastemakers *and a deft analyst of changing mores, is managing editor of* Harper's Magazine *and (by his own confession) has "frequently bowled over 200."*

ATELIER
TO
THE
EMPIRE

The ancients prized the sculpture from remote Aphrodisias;

then the tumultuous history of Asia Minor submerged it.

Now the brilliance of its art is coming to light again

The Roman emperors knew it well. In the city of Aphrodisias, beyond the Aegean Sea, there were artists—the best in the Empire. From here the Caesars eagerly sought the marble statuary that would soon adorn their new villas. From the ports of Ephesus or Miletus in Asia Minor, over a sea voyage of some thousand miles, Aphrodisias exported its art—and often its artists—to the imperial capital and beyond.

To see the remains of this once famed center of the classical province of Caria, you must follow a dusty route through the fertile valley of the Maeander River (now called the Menderes), in the southwestern Turkish province of Aydin, and up a steady climb. The road slowly becomes rough and stony, twisting and turning among olive groves and canyonlike stream beds. Looming large in the encircling mountain ranges is the jagged peak of Baba Dag. As you near its slopes an oasis of swaying poplars and pomegranate trees catches the eye—and, dimly at first, then startlingly, the white Ionic columns (see opposite) of Aphrodisias appear. A tiny hamlet called Geyre nestles with its tottering houses amid the relics of a dead city, once so influential in art that its designs have been found as far distant as Leptis Magna, the ancient seaport of Roman Africa.

These Ionic columns veiled by poplars were probably part of Aphrodisias's agora

Aphrodisias was more than a thousand miles from Rome

The marble image of Aphrodite (far left), recently unearthed near the site of her temple in Aphrodisias, resembles more the full-formed goddess of fertility associated with Asia Minor than the later Western patroness of love and beauty. Dating from c. A.D. 100, her apronlike tunic is decorated in the center with the Three Graces flanked by the heads of Zeus and Hera. Other new finds from classic Aphrodisias are the strong marble countenance of a magistrate or priest (left) and a couple united in death on their marble sarcophagus (above). The stadium of the city (opposite), had a seating capacity of some 30,000.

What made remote Aphrodisias so famous then? Only now is the full wealth of its artistic treasure coming to light, due to current excavations by a team of New York University archaeologists under the direction of Dr. Kenan T. Erim. They have uncovered testimony of the city's Hellenistic, Roman, and Byzantine history, and a mass of its renowned but long-forgotten statuary (see above).

Though Romans had sculptors much nearer at hand than those of Aphrodisias, so far across the sea, they turned to this city because, with its nearby supplies of excellent Carian marble, it had become the seat of a vigorous tradition of stone carving. And cosmopolitan Rome, always eager to garner treasures from its far-flung possessions, hardly tried to rival Aphrodisias; it simply bought up its work.

So it was that in the second and third centuries of the Christian era a far-reaching school of sculpture flourished at Aphrodisias and provided superb copies of Greek sculpture for Roman patrons, as well as its own original creations. Never shy, the Aphrodisians were among the few ancients to sign their pieces. Two dark-gray marble centaurs, now in the Capitoline Museum in Rome, are signed by the Aphrodisian sculptors Aristeas and Papias. Other sculptors who identified themselves as Aphrodisians were Flavius Chryseros, Flavius Zenon, and Flavius Andronicus, all testifying to the renown of their school.

Yet perhaps the most masterful creations of the sculptors of Aphrodisias are works recently found in their own home city, which often do not carry any signature. Exquisite reliefs were discovered partly by accident in 1956 and again in 1961 by the New York University team. They are parts of a monument honoring a certain Zoilos, a citizen of Aphrodisias, who is shown surrounded by a bevy of allegorical figures,

Demos (the People), Timé (Honor), and Polis (the City).

For a city once so splendid—bearing such a lovely name and dedicated to such a famous goddess—our ancient sources of information are relatively scanty. Perhaps the city's happiness is the cause of it all: *"Les gens heureux n'ont pas d'histoire."* Freya Stark applies the word "ease" to Aphrodisias, where "the contentment of the bourgeoisie can be recaptured," and whose history is "written in its landscape," endowed with "an open remoteness, a happiness of width and distance."

In its early days, Aphrodisias must have been closely connected with the cult of the goddess, then not yet known as Aphrodite, but called by some indigenous Carian name (the Carians being the pre-Greek occupants of what is now southwestern Turkey). The city's history must have begun about the third century B.C. Its fame and that of its goddess were

such by the early first century B.C. that the Roman dictator Sulla, always partial by family tradition to Aphrodite, sent an offering of a gold crown and a double axe to the goddess upon being promised power by an oracle. Having successfully resisted the Parthians, Aphrodite's city was rewarded by Julius Caesar and Augustus: it was declared inviolable and its temple invested with right of asylum; a senatorial decree of 39 B.C. declared it free and exempt from paying tribute to Rome. These rights were renewed by subsequent emperors.

Such imperial favor and patronage, together with peace and prosperity, brought Aphrodisias by the second century to its halcyon days as a religious and artistic center. Medicine, rhetoric, and philosophy flourished in its schools. In A.D. 200 Alexander of Aphrodisias was a popular lecturer on Peripatetic philosophy in Athens. Musical and dramatic contests were held every four years, the first prize in drama being

99

Remnants of ancient Aphrodisias have been casually incorporated into the houses of Geyre, the Turkish hamlet that survives on its site. At left inhabitants of Geyre walk obliviously past fragments of the marbles for which the city was once famous in the Roman world. Opposite: In the fields beyond, columns and capitals located near the presumed agora of Aphrodisias protrude from the fertile earth.

reserved for a tragedian and the second for an actor of the Old Comedy.

An extensive building program was inaugurated, contributions coming from prosperous local citizens. The magnificent stadium (see page 99), in the northwest sector of the site, one of the most imposing in the whole Mediterranean area, accommodated 30,000 spectators. The enchanting row of columns pictured on pages 96–97 is located in the midst of young poplar groves. Possibly they formed a part of the porticoes of the agora.

One of the gems of Aphrodisias, partly excavated last year by the N.Y.U. team, is a covered auditorium of which nine rows of semicircular marble seats are in excellent condition. It may have been used for the gathering of civic or religious bodies, or even for musical entertainment as suggested by its elaborate stage decoration of handsome statuary.

A major project of the N.Y.U. expedition has been the excavation of the Temple of Aphrodite, built in the second century A.D., in the heart of the city. Today its fourteen columns still stand despite the vicissitudes of centuries. The third century may have witnessed an earthquake of serious proportions. During the same time Aphrodisias was threatened by invading Goths. (It may have been then that the city was hastily surrounded by a system of fortifications, built out of the remains of the earthquake-damaged buildings. These walls, in large part still standing, were repaired in the mid-fourth century, or may have been erected only at that time.) With the coming of Christianity to Aphrodisias in the fourth

century, the Temple of Aphrodite was made into a church.

Last summer, following a thunderstorm, some curiously carved marble fragments were revealed in the foundations of a late wall outside the temple-basilica. When the wall was dismantled, the towering nine-foot image of Aphrodite (page 98) was brought to light, centuries after its burial by the pious Christian Fathers of Aphrodisias.

The importance of Aphrodisias did not diminish with the advent of Christianity. The city became the seat of a bishop in Byzantine times and could boast of many churches, often built quite independently of earlier constructions. Aphrodisias also shared in the ill fortune of Byzantine Asia Minor. Its decline and disappearance were accelerated with the Seljuk invaders and other incursions from the east between the eleventh and fourteenth centuries.

Judging from the tombstones in its cemetery, the village of Geyre must date back to the seventeenth or eighteenth century. Yet a strange harmony between past and present is found in the humble houses. In the shady courtyards stand gaping sarcophagi: some of them, used as troughs, catch the spring waters descending from Baba Dag. Others, decorated with clusters of grapes carved on their flanks and used as wine presses, echo under the trampling feet of farmers. If one tries to remind the villagers of the original purpose of these coffins, they shake their heads and silently point to the grapes and the garlands of fruits carved on the sides. And life, like the blood of Dionysus, gushes out of the container of death.

Marisol's Mannequins

A young Venezuelan juggles mood and materials to create a sculpture of wit and wry sophistication

When a Latin-American artist sculpts the Man on Horseback, one might reasonably expect either a political paean or a stinging satire. Yet neither is the case with the barrel-chested, four-wheeled steed opposite, soberly mounted by both George Washington and Simon Bolívar, and capable of blaring forth martial music from a transistorized phonograph concealed inside. It is the work of the Venezuelan Marisol Escobar, who is unawed by history or convention and approaches this subject —as she does most others—with amused affection and gentle mockery. Like the rest of her wood-and-paint portraits, it manages to be both child-like and sophisticated at once.

Marisol (so she signs her work) has come to her individualistic style, and to this country, only recently. Born in Paris of wealthy and nomadic Venezuelan parents, she arrived in the United States in 1950 at the age of twenty. She studied painting with the abstractionist Hans Hofmann for three years, and then decided to try sculpture. Her early efforts—some showed an indebtedness to the figurines of South American folk art— were small animated totems of bronze and terra cotta. Then in 1957, in one dramatic move, came the switch from the miniature to the monumental—effected, she says, when she saw "an old coffee grinder, one of those wooden ones with wheels." The tactile, humorous appeal of the grinder, the connotations of this familiar object seen out of context, took her by surprise. Soon she was hauling home great lengths of timber and old moldings from demolition sites, castoff baby carriages and furniture from secondhand shops.

Marisol assembles these "found" objects as the underpinnings of her work, sculpting, turning, refining them into the robust figures that are her specialty. From her kitchen sink come assorted toes, breasts, noses, fingers, and buttocks cast in plaster; from her closet, hats and sneakers or whatever the fashion may demand. To this mélange, in airy defiance of purists who would segregate the arts, she adds the two-dimensional

Top: Family
Center: The artist in her studio
Bottom: Self-portrait
Opposite: The Generals

SCULPTURES COURTESY STABLE GALLERY, N. Y.

artist's media of pigment and pencil: her own painting covers surfaces of her sculpture (see the family portrait on preceding page).

This juggling of medium and materials, this deceptively casual composition of "junk," puts Marisol in the tradition of *assemblage,* a movement with distinguished literary and artistic antecedents. Early in this century a generation of artists including Picasso and Braque began experimenting with constructions of actual objects—scraps of newspaper, cloth, metal, string—carrying to its logical extreme the nineteenth century's romance with realistically painted *trompe-l'oeil* still lifes. Dadaists enlarged upon this new freedom for their anti-culture art in the twenties. Today's *assemblagistes* continue to dismantle the day-to-day world, reordering it in such different forms as the crumpled-up automobiles of the French sculptor César and the exquisite cubby-hole constructions of the American Louise Nevelson.

Unlike most adherents of this mix-and-match tradition, however, Marisol denies any desire to polemicize against affluent society or Kleenex kulture. She is not the least disturbed by the comfortable amusement of visitors to the gallery in New York where her last exhibition was held. And if, in addition, her admirers choose to find in her work some spoof on the more solemn members of her fraternity, that may just be among her intentions, too. She herself is not telling.

Above: Zoot, *despite its square solidity,*
portrays the jazz saxophonist Zoot Sims.
Right: A portrait originally anonymous was
later named John, *after a noted prelate.*

DRAWINGS BY NICHOLAS SOLOVIOFF

ON THE HORIZON

Every nation in a sense invents its own past, if only by a process of selecting what to include in history and what to leave out. In this there may often be less of willful self-deception than of a genuine desire to make sense out of a national experience. Some things worked and some did not; some proved to lead into the future and some to be historical blind alleys, going nowhere. It would be natural, not to say inevitable, if the former loomed larger than the latter in the picture a country or a continent painted of itself.

In the case of Africa, perhaps the oldest continent man has known but also the newest to emerge into world-wide attention, one can almost watch the history-making process take place (see "Africa: The Face Behind the Mask," by Basil Davidson, on page 38). For long, Africa was thought to have no history, or no history worth speaking of, since it appeared to consist of little more than meaningless and savage tribal rivalries among peoples whom the main current of man's historical development seemed to have left behind. Africans themselves, as they became educated in the ways of the modern West, have often turned against their own past and spurned it as unworthy of attention from such Europeanized men and women as they, by their efforts, had become. They "forgot" how to dance and play the drums, and came to look upon African sculpture as barbarous and Africa's rich folklore as a collection of old wives' tales.

Then one by one the former colonies became independent African states, and the pendulum swung to the opposite extreme. For having a history, like having a budget deficit or a mission to the United Nations, is one of the privileges of nationhood; and, in their eagerness to acquire a past, some of the new African nations have at times been more enthusiastic than discriminating in their choice of historical raw materials. When the colony that had been called the Gold Coast came to pick a new name for itself, it chose Ghana—even though the ancient Negro empire of Ghana had been located to the northwest, far outside the borders of the Gold Coast. Something of the Ghanians' overexuberance in the pursuit of history is also evident in their murals (see "Who's Underdeveloped?" in HORIZON for January, 1963), which claim for Africans the invention of architecture, chemistry, the alphabet, and other modest achievements.

A certain stimulus to the remaking of African history has come from the revived interest in Africa on the part of American Negroes. They too had gone through a period —a much longer, less willing, and more dismal period—of separation from their ancestral sources and traditions. Now they could read a counterpart of their own struggle for equality into Africa's struggle for self-government; and they could hardly help but draw satisfaction from the sight of African statesmen, capped and robed, received as equals by the mighty of the earth. They too have therefore looked to the African past and asked much of it, sometimes far too much, in the way of dignity and reassurance. Some have turned to Africa in the hope, all too often vain, of identifying themselves fully with its dilemmas and aspirations. Others, in their accumulated bitterness, have embraced not only the Moslem faith but a sort of Pan-Africanism which improves on racism only by reversing it and invites fantasies of an Africa turning time backward in its hatred of the whites.

*T*o these and other wild oscillations in belief, Davidson provides a welcome corrective. He came originally to the subject of African history as a novelist and a journalist; in the latter capacity he had "covered" much of Africa and indeed uncovered the scandalous survival in modern times of an ancient abuse, the forced-labor system in Angola. When he turned to the African past, therefore, it was as a man himself immersed in today's Africa and impelled by its urgencies. In at least that sense he is a partisan of Africa, and his books—on the discoveries of modern archaeology there or on the slave trade—are impassioned and polemical in intent. When he writes, as he does here, of the current reappraisal of African history, he does so as someone who has played a major part in the very process he describes.

Davidson's dispelling of past misconceptions about Africa is thus both a comment on the present and a forecast of the future, and it can be especially salutary in a realm somewhat apart from art and history—that of speculative philosophy. There exists in Africa, as he points out, a sufficiently large stock of common metaphysical beliefs to enable one to speak of "a basic unity of culture." Until recently, if a single word had to be found for the source of that unity, the word would have been "animism"—or the conviction, crudely put, that all things animate and inanimate are possessed by spirits. Europeans in Africa have long observed, most often with despair, that this notion is so central to an African's existence that many years of Western education may leave it undisturbed. In some corner of his mind the suave Oxford-accented government minister may still feel the ghostly presence of his ancestors, and fear the juju man.

But now it is beginning to be realized that beneath the surface of such apparently irrational behavior is a fully developed philosophy—a "prescientific" one, as Davidson observes, but a nonetheless comprehensive and unified view of the world. For example, the Catholic missionary Father Placide Tempels—in an ingenious and highly original book called *La Philosophie Bantoue*—has demonstrated that the superficially simple pagan "animism" of Africans reflects a rich and in many ways sophisticated system of thought built around the concept of vital force. The Bantu believe that to exist at all is to possess force, and

that the force of various beings—men, animals, natural phenomena, inanimate objects, and the dead included—may increase or diminish as they influence each other; the sum of human wisdom is the knowledge of how this interaction takes place. Where Western thought has traditionally emphasized the static and permanent, African thought emphasizes the dynamic and ever-changing.

Africa has much to learn from the modern West, but as Western philosophy moves to recapture a sense of change, of the flow of nature as opposed to the rigid abstractions we make from it, we too have much to learn from Africa. "I see us," writes the South African Laurens van der Post in *The Dark Eye in Africa,* "as two halves designed by life to make a whole. . . . We need the good that is in the values of 'primitive' man in Africa. Vast arid stretches in our own bigoted culture can be made fertile again by opening our culture to his urgent awakening spirit. Between us I believe we can make civilization greater and life richer on earth than it has ever been. . . . Could we but see—white and black—how lucky we are to have found each other at this far crossroad in time. . . ." E.L.

THEATRE

Laugh Now, Pay Later

During the past ten to fifteen years it has become increasingly hazardous to laugh in the theatre. An entire generation of audiences has come of age since the stage last rocked to the innocent, unmotivated, and inconsequential merrymaking of *Three Men on a Horse* and *You Can't Take It with You.* For the contemporary playwright, humor is a tool—in fact, it has become one of his weapons. Nowadays we implicate ourselves by our laughter; more often than not, we are the victims of the jest and, as it were, hoist on our own guffaws.

The tactical use of humor is not new to the stage: one has only to recall the porter in *Macbeth* or the gravediggers in *Hamlet.* Such comic scenes and figures worked as catalysts for the tragedy to come; laughter relaxed the audience, opened its senses, and the blade struck home with the greater force. But Shakespeare did not contrive ludicrous deaths (there was, I admit, the malmsey-butt in *Richard III,* but it stood off stage and presumably Clarence was dead before ever he went into it); he did not mix absurdity with terror or hilarity with disgust. Early in the present era, Jean-Paul Sartre announced in *No Exit* that hell is other people; to that has been added more recently the observation that the ultimate cry of agony is laughter.

The new chimeras of the stage range from tragic farce (Eugène Ionesco's *Rhinoceros*) to slapstick horror (Samuel Beckett's *Endgame*), to lethal fantasy (Jean Genet's *The Balcony*). They were written in the knowledge of antic scarecrows frozen to the electric fence; in anticipation of a war that, not content with corpses in quantities beyond precedent, will produce sports—funny-looking people. Happy laughter presupposes a considerable confidence in the stability of custom (such that it won't be toppled by one unguarded shout) and a structure of values that is generally understood if not scrupulously observed. Gilbert and Sullivan were forever inveighing against the smugness of their society, but in fact only a society secure enough to be smug could have given them relevance (their operettas are not relevant today, only nostalgic). The speed with which we have been deteriorating as a society can perhaps be gauged by recalling the joyful caricature that animated *Of Thee I Sing*. The Eisenhower administration was easily as laughable as Hoover's, but by then we had so lost a sense of destiny that attempts to lampoon Ike and his entourage turned rancid. Humor, in fact, has become a tough business.

*B*ertolt Brecht was one of the earliest of the modern dramatists to bully his public with laughter. He took fullest possible advantage of the fact that anything presented in a state of unaccustomed nakedness—from a plucked chicken to an unfrocked priest—is ludicrous, and that the humor it generates is amoral. The subject Brecht chose again and again to display in its birthday suit was villainy; his plays are crowded with greed, lust, larceny, hypocrisy, stupidity, all parading around the stage in bland nudity, as though they were babies pink from their baths. The effect has been admirably demonstrated this winter in Eric Bentley's adaptation of *A Man's a Man*. Galy Gay, a laborer who is goodhearted almost to the point of simple-mindedness, is converted during eleven scenes of vaudeville into a compulsive military killer. What makes the play funny, in its grim, dangerous way, is that the British soldiers (the play is set in a place called India) who reconstruct Galy are easily his peers in transparent fecklessness. We laugh to see their boyish tricks and are left with our mouths hanging open when the blood begins to run. Brecht has a ferocious way of making funny faces at us and then, when we laugh, telling us sharply that we have a peculiar sense of humor. He seeks to unmask, thus, still another kind of villainy—that of irresponsibility.

Brecht was certainly a moralist; nevertheless the fault I have to find with this excellently ribald and circuslike production is that it so insistently wags the moral at us. Bent-

ley is a diligent student of Brecht and has, I am certain, good grounds for the tone he develops. But the director, John Hancock, might have ruled that the dose of admonishment prescribed by Brecht for a pre-World War II audience could be so large as to stupefy a generation sensitized to propaganda. We expect irony and don't require a "Now, students" tone to recognize when we are being exposed to it. It would have been better, perhaps, to play *A Man's a Man* "straight," trusting the grisly comedy to make its point. Nevertheless, this production is brutally funny—the dead and the damned, off on a carefree binge.

A much more advanced (I don't say better) use of laughter is on view in Arthur Kopit's *Oh Dad, Poor Dad, Mamma's Hung You in the Closet and I'm Feelin' So Sad*. The humor here is characterized by the title—there is nothing inherently funny about it; one laughs because it is so inappropriate that one doesn't quite know what else to do. This is another kind of bullying—the tactic of putting your opponent off balance by behaving in a way he has no possible reason to expect. The effect usually is to induce a nervous and debilitating giggle. It is good mental jujitsu, but in this case I am not persuaded that Kopit has a valid reason for tripping us up. I suspect that he enjoys watching people sprawl, and that is unamiable of him.

The way to deal with such a title as his is to cut it, as everyone does, to *Oh, Dad. . . .* And the way to deal with his very clever and totally disconcerting play is to define it as a homosexual version of *Little Lord Fauntleroy*. Because, although its significance may be baffling, its imagery is tiresomely clear: the giant Venus flytraps that snap at unwary males with fleshy, teeth-rimmed lips; mother's suitor, who is paralyzed by her sustained and suffocating kiss; the pet fish who eats kittens alive (curiously, the play contains no instance of cannibalism); the huge, homemade telescope with which the son confuses his girl caller; the enormous and chaotic collections of stamps, coins, books; and of course the corpse of Dad, which falls out of the closet and becomes entangled with sonny, who is timorously trying to lose his virginity with a possessive hussy on mamma's bed. The result of this sort of thing is that the in-group laughs gleefully at how killingly the author has worked private signals into his public script; and the out-group laughs hollowly in the realization that it has come to the wrong party. I admire Kopit's stagecraft, and I don't doubt the reality of his nightmare; but I hope that another time he will sublimate what's biting him enough to implicate a larger segment of his audience.

If you laugh at Edward Albee's *Who's Afraid of Virginia Woolf?*—and everyone does—you may come to accuse yourself of heartlessness. It devotes itself to a very long night in the living room of a university couple who torment each other with wit, or at least witticisms. Ostensibly, the source of their mutual viciousness lies in her contempt for a man less successful than her father and his revulsion against the means by which such success is attained. Another, much younger faculty couple is also present during the nightlong bout of drink and vivisection (a good deal of the laughter is engendered by their bewilderment at being under the knives of their hosts), and the husband of this pair is shown to represent the kind of cold-blooded calculation that does lead to departmental chairmanships. Nevertheless, I came to believe that the assassinating impulses of the main couple were compulsive, remote from real clashes of principle or character; they fought because they had been warped to fight. This does not invalidate the play, but it places a clinical limitation on its tragedy.

Albee is the most talented of the young American playwrights who have won wide attention in the past ten years. No one since Tennessee Williams has taken such sure and ruthless command of the stage. It troubles me that in his most ambitious play to date, and his first to be offered on Broadway, he is so severely a spectator of his own creation. To use an old-fashioned term, *Who's Afraid of Virginia Woolf?* lacks catharsis: at the end, it merely turns disconcertingly and inconclusively soft. And that, I think, is because the playwright is working from data rather than conviction. It seems that he cannot resolve what he did not instigate—which is common enough in life but not sufficient for art. In retrospect the heartlessness of the audience's laughter may be laid at the door of the playwright's neutrality. Asked to describe the play, one is forced to say: "It is about this man and this woman who. . . ." That is much too particular to justify the intensity of the evening's pain and horror (we do not go to the theatre to see accidents). It is not the way one would describe *A Doll's House*; for that matter, it is not the way one describes Albee's *The Death of Bessie Smith*. Only farce can limit itself successfully to the singular.

*A*lbee is a playwright who has come to Broadway after a considerable apprenticeship in the outlying houses. Herb Gardner, author of *A Thousand Clowns,* on the other hand, writes as though Broadway had invented him. This is his first play, but already he is master of that most salable gambit, the pulled punch. He tells us of an individualist who rebels against the conforming, conniving, humiliating mores of American business life. How, then, can American businessmen and their wives, who make up almost the whole of Gardner's audience, laugh at his jibes with quite unguarded pleasure and march out of the theatre with their faces creased by smiles? Because the rebel is pictured in terms of such immature and irrelevant naughtiness that rebellion is plainly seen as kid stuff; and because his business-obsessed brother, who candidly admits that he cheats a little and cringes a little, is applauded (I mean, everybody claps) for doing the best he can. Phooey! Gardner pretends that rebellion is a stroll up Park Avenue on a Sunday morning, to shout taunts at the blank windows; at the same time he defines real grown-up life as providing the right toys for the wife and kiddies and never mind if you cut a few corners and lick a few boots—who doesn't? He must know better (he's smart enough to write a very negotiable play), but he gives his audience a painless laugh at themselves and a warm feeling in the belly. I predict a most successful career.

From here on we can move a little faster. Jean Kerr's *Mary, Mary* and *Take Her, She's Mine* by Phoebe and Henry Ephron are routine laugh machines of the sort that are always around and never remembered. They are not imitations of life; they are imitations of other plays. The former concerns a divorced couple who discover that they really love each other best of all; the latter is about a father who must learn that his daughter is a big girl now. The audience laughs because, well-educated in such fare, it knows that certain words ("virgin," for example) and certain situations (a man trying to maintain his pugnacity while under the influence of sleeping pills) have been tested and found risible by the most astute box-office practitioners. There is nothing wrong with plays of this sort—the theatre is a store as well as an art, and there are never enough artists around to keep all the shelves filled. You could maintain, in fact, that workmen like Mrs. Kerr and the Ephrons hold the franchise for the much slower and less reliable real playwrights. I found *Mary, Mary* amusing and *Take Her, She's Mine* embarrassing, but that is accidental and the next time around the situation might be reversed.

Finally, and in contrast to the general situation described at the beginning of this piece, the four-man British revue *Beyond the Fringe* offers a wit that is sharp, contemporary, and satiric, but which can be laughed at with relative impunity. That is so especially for an American audience. The kaleidoscope of accents is a wonder to hear, but it scarcely sorts out into anything we can identify as "ours" or "theirs"; and though we may be able to sense the other nuances of class, they are not details that arouse any personal response. We may suspect that C. P. Snow does not enjoy being named the exemplar of the innocuous Briton, but it is not a point on which we would rise to cheer or to stalk from the theatre.

The four recent university graduates who wrote and who perform these skits (none considers himself a stage professional and all have other careers to pursue) are gloriously acute observers of absurdity, pomposity, and sham, and hilariously accurate mimics of their victims. England still retains a high degree of tolerance for eccentricity, and the satire in *Beyond the Fringe* focuses less on the venalities of society than on the crotchets of individualistic extremes—from Prime Minister Macmillan to a coal miner with aspirations to abstract thought. Low Church obfuscators, elderly and inarticulate clubmen, dotty university philosophers, civil-defense enthusiasts, are the targets. An

American audience laughs because these cartoons are inherently funny (and because Messrs. Bennett, Cook, Miller, and Moore are astute and resourceful clowns); an English public would be more apt to feel that its own observations were being brilliantly materialized. But I doubt that even in London many spectators found themselves caught in the line of fire. This limits the bite of the satire, but it also endows the revue with a combination of wit and good nature that is rare to the point of being phenomenal on our stage.

It is hard not to envy the British for being able to turn out such a work as *Beyond the Fringe,* impossible not to wonder whether there are any recent Harvard or Yale graduates who could handle the Bible and Shakespeare with such witty familiarity, could observe their elders and their times with as much irony and as little hostility. England today has its corrosive comedians (Osborne, say, or Pinter), and France nourishes the almost lethal jesting of Genet. But the older societies also support a sophisticated geniality of the sort represented by *Beyond the Fringe* or Giraudoux. Here in America we seem to swing between a grin that is all teeth and a guffaw that is decerebrated. We have always been a very funny people, full of pranks and hyperbole, but wit has largely evaded us. And now that we find ourselves the rather youthful custodians of man's fate, it is a real question whether we shall ever learn to smile.

ROBERT HATCH

MOVIES

Adrift on a Sea of Gore

Spiritual themes are the occasion for the goriest and most violent scenes in the movies today. Movie makers, when they have an obviously good thing on hand, like Liberty (*Spartacus*), Chivalry and Honor (*El Cid*), or Our Lord (*Ben Hur* and now *Barabbas*), can really pour it on; they drench us in blood and blame the barbarous past for it. But the Roman crowds whose heartlessness makes us shudder didn't have the best seats in the house. We do.

The cunning work of the camera in close-ups allows us to watch these torments in privileged intimacy. Under the stands, after the chariot race, we see Messala shivering cruelly as he dies. We watch the face of Jack Palance as he begs the crowd for mercy just before Anthony Quinn (Barabbas) and his sword put an end to his sufferings. We

derive some gratification from this violence, *and* we are able to congratulate ourselves on our superiority to these frightful pagans. We are invited to enjoy the passions of the murderer and the blessings of innocence and enlightenment at the same time. We can't lose. No one can lose. All impulses can be gratified at once, and the thing is profitable as well. This can only be called all-purpose spiritual materialism. Here is a phenomenon not restricted to movies; in our public life religious and quasi-religious personalities have concocted dismal mixtures of piety and opportunism. We have been asked to swallow many a queer dose.

*D*ino De Laurentiis, who produced *Barabbas,* Richard Fleischer, who directed it, and Christopher Fry, who adapted it from the novel *Barabbas* by the Nobel Prize-winning author Pär Lagerkvist, have commemorated the release of the movie in an illustrated book, *Barabbas: The Story of a Motion Picture.* Here they tell us solemnly how it all happened. It seems that the making of this picture greatly affected them spiritually and gave them as artists an unforgettable experience, like the experience of Barabbas himself after he had witnessed the Crucifixion. Do they really believe this? Apparently they do. "*Barabbas*," explains De Laurentiis, "offered more than the usual problems of transferring a novel to the visual medium of the screen, for it is the story of one man's search for faith and truth laid against the most spectacular period in history. We had to combine these two vastly different elements but we believe we have succeeded in producing what might be called the first 'intimate spectacle' in motion picture history."

All the principals—Messrs. Fleischer, Fry, Quinn, and De Laurentiis—make many bows and obeisances before the creative superiority of Pär Lagerkvist. De Laurentiis bends so hard that we begin to have orthopedic fears for his back. He quotes the pronouncement of the historian Giovanni Papini, author of a book on Jesus, on *Barabbas.* "It is not a historical novel, nor is it a romantic novel; it is an intellectual poem." Trembling, De Laurentiis accepts this intellectual poem as a business risk. And he tells us that no one but Christopher Fry, a devout Christian playwright of great refinement (*A Sleep of Prisoners; The Boy with a Cart; Thor, with Angels*) could possibly do the script.

At this point one is tempted to say this enterprise is simply high-minded bunk, pious cheating, the same old racket. But then reading over the statements of De Laurentiis and the others, one detects no evidence of deliberate cheating. Throughout, the attitudes of producer, director, and writer are consistently earnest, respectful, serious, humble without exaggeration. There is something extraordinarily touching about such evident good faith. Could it be that the producer and his associates have confused what they set out to do with what they have done?

The critic Lucien Maury says of Lagerkvist's novel that

it is austere and "of a form that has been pared down to essentials." According to the description of Lagerkvist, this ruffian Barabbas, in whose place Jesus died, was a stubborn man, a creature entirely of this world, a rudimentary rationalist whose heart was closed to awe. Divine mystery would not let him alone but followed him throughout his life. Barabbas died in Rome, on a cross, saying to the darkness, "To thee I deliver up my soul."

De Laurentiis, Fleischer, and Fry have made sure they would not fall into a similar error. The darkness they work in is, to be sure, the darkness of the theatre, but they have taken particular care to give their souls a better orientation. They do not resist the allure of "the most spectacular period in history," and there is nothing restrained or austere about their "intimate spectacle." The idea of an intimate spectacle goes down a little hard. Still, we have been trained in our time to get down all sorts of stuff. We know it is the usual thing for modern artists, particularly in the motion-picture industry, where great wealth and technical resources afford original means for deranging the senses, to teach us new tricks and realign our sensibilities. For this, after our first resistance has been overcome, we are often grateful. If they tell us, in this era of eighty-minute circumnavigations of our planet, that they are about to put Golgotha and the Circus Maximus in our laps, we had better not object. Reserving judgment, therefore, we go on to see what De Laurentiis and his company have wrought.

We see first what they have done with the novel. There is not much blood in this book. (Lagerkvist's imagination is not stirred to extremes by "the most spectacular period in history." A reflective, private man, undevoted to the acquisition of money, he no doubt prefers the Greeks.) But there are lakes of blood in this picture, just as in the less "intimate" spectaculars. The extras, selected from the cast of thousands, die horribly, covered with *salsa di pomidoro* (the picture was made in Italy). In addition to all the blood, the producers have added an intimate mine disaster and set off an intimate series of sulphurous explosions. The slaves stagger, scream as they are burned, are buried alive, or succumb bleeding under fallen beams. This last episode is not very different from that of the sea battle in *Ben Hur,* a movie adapted from the far less austere novel by General Lew Wallace. In the matter of sex the producers of *Barabbas* have also allowed themselves several liberties. The humble harelipped girl who appears in the novel is transformed into the beautiful Rachel (Silvana Mangano) and forced to submit to the rough embrace of Anthony Quinn.

But Quinn, whose testimony is added to the rest in the publicity book, seems highly satisfied with the way things have been done. He had had his doubts about Biblical films, he says. "Too often, I had found, they were simply an excuse for illustrating sin and sex in a lurid manner." And he had been about to turn down the invitation of De Laurentiis when he learned that the script would be written by Christopher Fry, a writer who could be trusted to deliver a great spiritual message to an international public. Well, a picture without a beautiful woman or two is hardly imaginable, and the woman, once introduced, can't very well be ignored. Miss Mangano is ill-used only once and this—as spectaculars, intimate and otherwise, go—shows remarkable restraint. She is stoned to death in a pit.

But Quinn was on to something. Everything that we are spared in lasciviousness we are given in violence. Christopher Fry has, for instance, expanded the part of Sahak, the Christian slave (Vittorio Gassman) who suffers an obscure martyrdom in the novel. In the movie he and Barabbas are brought to Rome and enrolled in the gladiatorial school. Fleischer explains that he used "the spectacle of the arena and the gladiators simply as a means of developing the character of Barabbas, not as an end in itself. It would have been silly," he says, "to ignore such things for they were a part of the life and times of ancient Rome."

That the Circus was there all the while is perfectly true. Still, a good many people did manage to stay out of it. Saint Paul, who encountered some of the worst evils of the Empire, did not have to attend the gladiatorial college; nor did Pär Lagerkvist seem to feel the omission silly. Perhaps it is nearer the truth that many pictures rich in spiritual content also get in far larger amounts of pain and bloodshed than they require to float the message.

*N*o one would dream of scolding a movie for being a movie. There is nothing new about the passive pleasure of virtue when it beholds the wicked in hell—a very ancient form of entertainment, many centuries older than colored films and caramel-corn. Therefore *let* this martyr Rachel have lovely legs. *Let* the effects people have a field day with a genuine eclipse, as noonday darkens on Calvary. *Let* the mine blow up and burn and bury the slaves. *Let* us have the gladiators at school training with the swinging spiked ball, the trident, and the net. *Let* Jack Palance show his white teeth in sadistic glee à la Richard Widmark as he rides down poor clods in his chariot. *Let* the Italian extras fall down, gushing tomato paste. We are used to all this and find it easy to understand.

What is difficult to explain, however, is the sincerity of the company, the spiritual purpose, the reverence, the dedication, and the lump in the throat. Do these people believe what they are saying? Are they aware of any hypocrisy? Perhaps De Laurentiis and the company are, and yet *are not,* being truthful. Just as the spectator enjoys both the cruel act and the purity of innocence, so it is possible that the artists are able to combine spiritual intentions with hokum.

Like their entertainment, their problem has a long and ancient pedigree; it is the problem of reconciling religious and practical activities. Practical people are often enraptured by the idea of a spiritual enterprise, and are so carried away by the declaration of their high aims that what they actually do scarcely matters. Many people nowadays are too sophisticated to be caught in an obvious hypocrisy and have learned instead to put out a sort of aromatic fog of purple vapor in which everything seems honest, and nothing need be definitely untrue.

SAUL BELLOW

BOOKS

Greetings from Goethe's Land

Loathsome and brilliant, murderous and funny, incoherent and compelling, eloquent and obscene, implausible and alive, such is *The Tin Drum.* Published in Germany in 1959 as *Die Blechtrommel,* it is the first novel of a talented and versatile German artist, poet, and playwright, Günter Grass, who is thirty-six this year. It has now been translated (a difficult job, I imagine) by Ralph Manheim and published by Pantheon: a big book of 575 pages, forty-six chapters organized in three large sections. Some American readers will never open it because they are repelled by the coarse and cruel side of Germany, which *The Tin Drum* displays with rare gusto. Some will start it and throw it away in disgust. But those who read it to the finish, through alternate fits of admiration and repulsion, will think about it for many days and will never forget it.

The plot is impossible. Its hero is impossible. Its telling is impossible. Still, we believe a nightmare while we dream it.

It is the life story of a freak, a hunchbacked dwarf, named Oskar Matzerath. Born in 1924, he is thirty years old when he begins, lying in a mental hospital, to look back over his career and write his autobiography. He is not unhappy, for the authorities allow him to beat his drum several hours a day; he is reasonably comfortable, for he is rich and has friends to visit him and bring him presents; and he has plenty of time. Two years earlier he was arrested for murder: although he had not committed the crime, he supplied a witness who gave evidence against him, took to flight, was arrested, and although seemingly guilty, was declared insane. (When Interpol picked him up in Paris, he said, not for the first time, "I am Jesus.") The case may be reopened and Oskar cleared; but he is still insane, and shrinks from the prospect of being released into a world where he will have to start his ministry and gather disciples.

The tale of his life is insensate and horrible. His growth was arrested at the age of three by a fall down the cellar stairs. (In his insanity Oskar boasts that he deliberately dived down headfirst, to avoid growing up and becoming a grocer like his father; at first you almost believe him.) Thereupon he became a drummer and a screamer. For hours every day he beat his drum. When they took it away from him, he screamed. And his screams smashed glasses, broke windows, intimidated all who tried to control him. Not that he was an imbecile. He learned to write, to read: his favorite literature was Goethe's *Elective Affinities* and a book on Rasputin's sexual adventures. He grew in cleverness, if not in stature and grace. True, the other children played tricks on him, such as making him drink frog-and-urine soup; and his mother died after a surfeit of eels and sardine oil; but Oskar survived. He even managed to beget a son on a girl bedfellow, whom he stimulated by giving her fizz powder mixed with his own spittle.

No, he did not remain a child at heart; but he kept the childish advantages of insignificant smallness and apparent innocence. So, when he broke up Nazi rallies by playing his diabolical drum and throwing the demonstrators out of step, he was too tiny to be found. When the Free City of Danzig became the earliest battlefield of the Second World War, he was actually in the Polish Post Office at the moment that the Germans stormed it; all its defenders were shot, but Oskar, looking babyish and cute, was let go. When the war grew intense, he became a stunt performer traveling with a troupe of midget clowns and entertaining the German armed forces. When the Russians entered Danzig, he contrived to get them to shoot his father, and then escaped to the west on a refugee train floored with vomit and feces. (At this point, Oskar grew a few inches taller and produced a doubtless symbolic hump.)

After the war, he still managed to exist, as a black marketeer, a tombstone cutter, an artist's model, a jazz musician, and finally a virtuoso drummer. But his midget friend Bebra died; the nurse, Sister Dorothea, whom he had loved, was murdered. He was lonely; he had nothing left but Sister Dorothea's severed finger; he feigned a confession of guilt, and so his career, with a sharp bump of anticlimax, ended.

*A*t first sight this monstrous book looks as though it might be a satire on the life of Germany during the Hitler era, the war, and the postwar boom. Its hero has a German name and thinks in German. He is born just about the time that Hitler was released from prison and refounded the Nazi party. He disrupts its demonstrations with impunity; takes a cynically passive part in the first combat of the war; entertains the garrison of the Atlantic Wall on the eve of the Overlord invasion; is the inspiration, and indeed the deity, of a gang of young hooligans who outdo and intimidate the Hitler Youth; falls into squalor with the defeat of

Hitler's Mad Drummer

"There was once a toystore owner; his name was Sigismund Markus and among other things he sold tin drums lacquered red and white. Oskar was the principal taker of these drums, because he was a drummer by profession and was neither able nor willing to live without a drum. For this reason he hurried away from the burning synagogue in the direction of Arsenal Passage, for there dwelt the keeper of his drums; but he found him in a state which forever after made it impossible for him to sell tin drums in this world.

"They, the same firemen whom I, Oskar, thought I had escaped, had visited Markus before me; dipping a brush in paint, they had written "Jewish Sow" obliquely across his window in Sütterlin script; then, perhaps disgusted with their own handwriting, they had kicked in the window with the heels of their boots, so that the epithet they had fastened on Markus could only be guessed at. Scorning the door, they had entered the shop through the broken window and there, in their characteristic way, they were playing with the toys.

"I found them still at play when I, also through the window, entered the shop. . . . One had drawn his dagger. He was cutting dolls open and he seemed disappointed each time that nothing but sawdust flowed from their limbs and bodies. . . .

"Markus had escaped from their rage. When they went to see him in his office, they did not knock, they broke the door open, although it was not locked.

"The toy merchant sat behind his desk. As usual he had on sleeve protectors over his dark-grey everyday jacket. Dandruff on his shoulders showed that his scalp was in bad shape. One of the SA men with puppets on his fingers poked him with Kasperl's wooden grandmother, but Markus was beyond being spoken to, beyond being hurt or humiliated. . . .

"There was once a drummer, his name was Oskar. When they took away his toy merchant and ransacked the shop, he suspected that hard times were in the offing for gnomelike drummers like himself. And so, in leaving the store, he picked out of the ruins a whole drum and two that were not so badly injured, and hung them round his neck. . . . Outside, it was a November morning. Beside the Stadt-Theater, near the streetcar stop, some pious ladies and strikingly ugly young girls were handing out religious tracts, collecting money in collection boxes, and holding up, between two poles, a banner with an inscription quoted from the thirteenth chapter of the First Epistle to the Corinthians. 'Faith . . . hope . . . love. . . .' "   —*from Günter Grass,* The Tin Drum

the Third Reich, and rises again as part of what they call the "Economic Miracle." True enough, as far as that goes. This is a modern perversion of *Simplicissimus* (1669), the German satiric romance about the orphan brought up by a hermit, who strays into the horrors of the Thirty Years' War and views them with the amazed eyes of an innocent.

Some European critics, working a little closer to the bull, have declared that *The Tin Drum* is a satire on the German national character as a whole. Little Oskar has no proper education, and could not attend the most demanding and rewarding of German schools, the *Gymnasium*; in fact, he read only two or three books. Yet his literary style is versatile and elegant: powerful in rhetoric, seductive in description—he can even imitate James Joyce. Symbolic, of course; it means that the Germans are highly intelligent people who have always lacked a real education, does it not? Or that they are intellectual giants and moral dwarfs?

*B*ut *The Tin Drum* is less than that, and more. Some of the most important aspects of Hitler's Germany are underemphasized or omitted. The regimentation of life; the mass slaughter of the concentration camps; the relentless activity of the Gestapo: these are scarcely mentioned and little satirized. The long effort of the war years, 1941, 1942, 1943, 1944, passes by in a few dozen pages. Besides, a great deal of the book's national feeling is not German but Slavic. Oskar (like his creator Günter Grass) was born in the frontier city then called Danzig, now known as Gdańsk; and he is at least part Slav. His maternal grandmother, the first person we meet, is a Kashube—one of a small group of coastal Slavs allied to but not identical with the Poles; so is her husband, Joseph Koljaiczek; and, naturally, Oskar's mother. His legal father is Alfred Matzerath, a Rhenish German; but Oskar, with some reason, suspects his mother of having conceived him by her cousin Jan Bronski, which would make him wholly non-German in blood. And he has something of an obsession, not with Germany, but with Poland. Almost the only truly romantic dream-figures in his mind (doomed though they may be) are the Polish cavalrymen. *"Deutschland über alles"* and the Horst-Wessel song are scarcely heard, even in parody; but at least twice we hear Oskar wildly drumming *"Jeszcze Polska Nie Zginęla"*—the Polish national anthem, "While still we live, Poland is not lost!"

From this point of view, then, *The Tin Drum* is a bitter fantasy on the life of the hybrid, who belongs to two different cultures and feels at home in neither—like James Joyce, caught between Saxon England and Celtic Ireland. It is easy to see why, by a purposeful misunderstanding, Oskar betrayed his putative father the German to the Russian invaders and, with Joycean selfishness, betrayed his real father the Pole to the German Home Guard. There will be more books like this, as the crossing and intermingling of races and cultures continues to increase.

The chief import of the novel, however, is neither nationalist satire nor the torment of lost identity. It is misanthropy, hatred, the wish to shock and nauseate the reader. The book is full of cruelty—witnessed by Oskar, inflicted on Oskar, inflicted by Oskar, and gloatingly described. Often the cruelty is funny, but in a grotesque way, so that we feel guilty for enjoying it. Oskar's friend Truczinski, infatuated by the beautiful figurehead of a ship, attempts to make love to it with the help of a double-edged axe and kills himself. The homosexual greengrocer Greff, wearing his scoutmaster's uniform, hangs himself in a contraption which, when he is cut down, releases a funereal drum roll of falling potatoes. Corporal Lankes, guarding the Atlantic Wall, machine-guns five stray nuns on the beach because they might be disguised British troops; meanwhile a clown acrobat alleviates the situation by playing a jazz record and standing on his head.

To Christian readers the most offensive thing in the novel will be, as it was intended to be, the blasphemy. Not only does Oskar hang his drum round the neck of a statue of the infant Jesus and challenge him to start drumming; not only do the hooligans put Oskar on the knees of a statue of Mary and perform a Mass in front of him; but eventually we see that Oskar thinks of himself as a contemporary Jesus whose mission has still to begin. And there are hints and consonances, equally blasphemous, throughout.

Blasphemy, nauseating descriptions of perverted eating and drinking, cruelty; the scream that shatters glass and destroys property ("property is theft"); the drum that destroys logic and calls up crazy images—all these combine into one major pattern, destructive anarchism. The message from the tin drum played by the maniac dwarf is simple, and is not so unlike Hitler's final scream: "Destruction to the world that will not follow Me!"

*I*f, as you read a book, you feel that the author hates you and all the fabric of your life, that his chief purposes in writing are to communicate to you his loathing and his scorn, and to shock you so radically that you will never fully recover or wholly forget, then he is a literary anarchist. In Henry Miller's two *Tropics,* between passages in which he uses terms of rancid vulgarity to describe the degraded practices of himself and his friends, he breaks into savage, almost incoherent monologues like the curses of Timon, calling down destruction upon mankind. Oaths and obscenities scattered through ordinary prose narrative are intended, just as a foul word scrawled on a wall, as a verbal blow aimed at all who read it.

The Tin Drum is an important novel in this new mood. The sweet old optimistic anarchism of Peter Kropotkin and his followers will never die as long as there are kind hearts and simple minds. But from now on we shall see more and more purely destructive anarchism. Grass grew

up in a generation that was utterly disgusted with all ideologies—political, religious, moral: in fact, he is far more bitter about Catholic Christianity than he is about the Nazis. In addition, there are many sensitive spirits who feel that organization is too much with us; that the state, the law, and systematic interference with individual life are becoming tyrannies, even if their rule is gentle in method and is intended to be beneficial in result. Some of these enter the escapist nihilism of drug addiction and rootless beatnik living. But some, like Luis Buñuel with his filmed images of cruelty and degradation,* and like Oskar with his relentless drum and his resistless scream, become the true nihilists with a single aim, of which they are perhaps not fully conscious: the annihilation of humanity.

GILBERT HIGHET

CHANNELS

The 21-inch Smokescreen

LeRoy Collins, once governor of Florida and more recently high potentate of the National Association of Broadcasters, rose in public not long ago and ostentatiously turned his back on a hundred forty million dollars a year in television revenues, or at least on a very large portion thereof. Specifically, Mr. Collins chastised the broadcasting industry for its dedicated efforts to seduce the youth of our land into cultivating an addiction to cigarettes. In view of what we are beginning to know about cigarette smoking, said Mr. Collins, this was foul play and unbefitting. He proposed that the industry do something about it.

This should lead no one to feel a deep sense of concern for the well-being of the broadcasting industry, which will take care of itself. There were no signs of a general rally to Mr. Collins's standard. Most of his colleagues, with one degree of politeness or another, advised their beloved leader to turn blue, implying that they were making a good thing out of snuggling up to the young in behalf of the gasper trade and, in the absence of *force majeure,* intended to go right on doing so. At the last reading, the television industry was still engaged in advertising cigarettes during intermissions of sports events and feeble-minded situation comedies, where the young are known to gather.

My condolences go—somewhat prematurely, I am sure —not to the television industry but to the cigarette indus-

*See "Movies: Buñuel's Unsparing Vision" by Saul Bellow, in HORIZON for November, 1962.

try, which is now bedeviled from every side. It has been difficult enough for the magnates to withstand the barrage laid down by physicians and surgeons. But now they are in the position of a quarterback who is tackled from behind by the coach—the attack comes from within. The hand that feeds $400,000 a day into television, most of it during the afternoon and early evening, is being bitten right up to the wrist. Even the advertising industry, with a solid 15 per cent stake in the hundred forty million, is making vague noises that indicate a reluctance to read Mr. Collins out of the club just yet. *Advertising Age,* for example, has announced that it took a great deal of courage for "Governor Collins to suggest tampering with $140,000,000 of cigarette advertising in order to protect young people from possible health hazards." One would have to go far to find a more immoral statement, but for the ad industry it is equivalent to a clarion cry.

Life has been hard for the cigarette manufacturers for a good many years now. They are faced with the necessity of selling a product universally conceded to be noxious to a nation of the most determined valetudinarians in the civilized world. As anyone who follows the ads must recognize, we live our lives out in the desperate pursuit of health. There is no cavity, whether sinus, dental, or of the more majestic dimensions, that we do not regularly penetrate with medicament. We engage in a dogged search for fats that are rich in poly-unsaturates. We brush (to quote one soapmaker) "every chance we get," which calls up a tender image of American home life with mother, father, and the infants foaming at the mouth in concert, hour-in and hour-out. We gobble pills, some with buffering, some without. And when at last the moment comes that, panting with exertion, we can tend our health no longer, we relax with Ben Casey or Dr. Kildare.

*T*his is a tough market to saturate with cigarettes. It works only because most adults are addicted and the only choice they have is a choice between brands. They can't stop even if they want to, so they smoke, and eat more poly-unsaturates to make up for it. But this will remain a stable situation only if the trade can keep addicting the young—and it has to be the young because it is very hard to addict a man after thirty. He lacks the cast-iron constitution of the adolescent, and is likely to get dizzy before the habit can take hold.

Yet the structure threatens to crumble. It is not only that LeRoy Collins has become sharper than a serpent's tooth and *Advertising Age* commends him for it. Brothers in the trade itself are whetting their knives. Some months back I wrote in this column my surprise that cigar manufacturers had forborne to plunge stilettos into the bowed backs of their colleagues across the street. They forbear no longer. "Peace of mind in every puff," says the Robert Burns commercial, and that should be clear enough.

The same company, by the way, is also engaged in an effort to convince the ladies of the delights that reside in the five-cent cigar. So far the attack is discreet. The lady never does get to puff on a panatela. But "shouldn't a gentleman offer a *tiparillo* to a lady?" an assortment of glamourous dames asks the television audience—all the while eyeing a stogie with the passion usually reserved for mink coats and Rock Hudson. It takes me back to the days when George Washington Hill urged the ladies to "Reach for a Lucky instead of a sweet"—later modified to "Reach for a Lucky instead" when the candy combine howled. Well, it worked for Luckies, and for all I know it may work for Robert Burns. The ladies smoke cigars in Denmark, and I never heard anyone complain.

*W*hile gentlemen are chivalrously winning ladies by means of cigars, their television juniors are, it seems, going about the same thing more bluntly, and in this caviling mood I should like to enter a protest against a recent Ford commercial, which drives home the point that the best way to pick up girls on the street is to drive slowly alongside in a Ford convertible. I have never before been disturbed about efforts to convince boys (or girls) that the most efficient way to entice girls (or boys) into their arms is to eat, wear, wash in, smear on, or inhale some readily available commercial product. About 90 per cent of all advertising is some kind of variation on this simple theme, and it always struck me as harmless, perhaps because in my own experience it simply never seemed likely that a little dab would do it.

The Ford commercial is quite different, because it is probably quite accurate, and would be even more unquestionably accurate if the convertible were a Cadillac. This appears to me to be the wrong basis upon which to sell automobiles, and for the life of me, I don't know why. It bothers me, that's all. I may see an analyst about it, and then again, I may buy a convertible. All in all, I am a soul in torment.

While in torment, I might allude briefly to what appears to be a sudden proliferation of television commercials selling dog food. (Some very good commercials, by the way.) Are there really that many dogs eating out of cans? I always thought people fed them leftover Spam. Or, as with Robert Burns, is this a subtle attempt by pet-food manufacturers to widen their market? Can I expect ultimately to see a commercial in which a dog-lover muses, "Shouldn't a dog offer some Gravy Train to his master?" I don't mind—anything that helps the economy helps us all.

So much for the picture-tube. I had intended to write also about *Beverly Hillbillies,* but I am resisting the temptation in the hope that it will have vanished by the time this appears in print. It now appears to be the most popular program on television, leading me to believe I am likely to vanish long before it does.   STEPHEN WHITE

The Culture of the Non-Hotel

By JOSEPH MORGENSTERN

*W*ith the removal of cabin partitions and the suppression of certain amenities, the SS *United States,* designed and built by visionaries, can be converted in one week into a troop ship. The new hotels going up in this country, flagships of their own far-flung fleets, are contrived more ingeniously still. With no changes in structure or managerial philosophy, they can be converted into barracks.

They are, these soaring slabs, exemplars of a radical development in hostelry. Like military installations, they are spare if not downright Spartan, and greatly concerned with efficiency. They are less concerned with personal service, encouraging self-service as a healthy—and efficient—form of self-expression. They have taken a leaf from the register of the motel, or garage with guest facilities, in leaving clients to their own devices and providing plenty of devices to leave them to.

Accordingly, the new American hotel is amply equipped with automatic elevators, television sets, conditioned air, and ice-making machines. The provision of ice cubes has become a hallmark of hotel service, and new machines can provide, in any given twenty-four-hour period, some forty pounds of efficient, multipurpose cubes, which can be used in beverages, carved into little icicles, or melted down, if need be, into safe drinking water.

But gone are the frivolities of yesteryear. Banished is the chambermaid who would come into the room in the evening to turn back the bedcovers, a feat that can be performed efficiently by the guest himself. Gone is the terry-cloth bathrobe, replaced by the oversized hand towel. Gone is the vast, tidal bathtub, replaced by a hygienic stall shower with multiple squirts. Dismissed are the bootblacks, those silent elves who cleaned shoes left in the corridors at night. Leave your shoes outside the door in a new American hotel and there they will remain for the night, foot-loose and polish-free. At least they will not be stolen: the staff is too small to include a shoe stealer.

This revolution can be attributed in part to a subsidiary revolution in hotel management and the standardization resulting from chain operations. Establishments like the Summit and the Americana, two of the newest to sprout in New York City during the current hotel-building boom, are run by a subsidiary of a movie company that is razing some of its neighborhood theatres and replacing them with high-rental apartment houses and high-flung hotels.

These Loew's hotels, together with their sister motels, represent the triumph of the businessman over the *hôtelier de métier.* The hosteler of the past had to be an acute businessman in his own right, but he knew that the greatest efficiency could be got from human beings, not machines,

and he remembered that the essence of a hotel is personal, knowledgeable service. Machines need not be tipped, but neither can they be depended upon to supplant people.

The conscientious *hôtelier* also built his establishment to last; inside, his furniture and decoration were durable. The Summit, on Lexington Avenue, is just twenty months old, and already stands in need of repair. The vinyl material that covers the wall plaster is buckled and lumpy; carpeting is soiled and irregularly fitted; fixtures are dented or broken. No one has ever come upon a more efficient way of keeping hotel supply houses in business. The Middle-Miami-Beach architecture has given rise to the now standard observation that "the hotel is all right but it's a long way to the ocean."

A publicity man who spent a week at the Summit recalls the experience vividly. The walls were so thin he and his wife ascertained that the man next door was named John, and that he dropped three ice cubes into his glass before pouring a drink. There was no shortage of ice cubes.

Room service was hardly memorable: "One night we ordered *châteaubriant* for two. An hour later two uniformed chauffeurs rolled it into our room under a huge silver bell, as if it were some rare delicacy from a foreign land. It was, in fact, London broil, and they had forgotten the mushrooms. My wife called downstairs to protest the omission and the room-service operator said: 'I'm sorry, hon, but the chef gets so busy.' We never got mushrooms."

When no clean pillowcases were forthcoming one morning, the publicity man and his wife were advised, pragmatically enough, to use dirty ones. An order of tea with cream elicited a pot of tea accompanied by a carton of milk, for which there was an additional charge. The Summit boasts a European-style concierge, but guests have trouble finding him at his little European-style concierge's counter. One disenchanted customer dismissed him as a "foreign bell captain."

Over on Seventh Avenue, the Americana is billed as the world's tallest hotel. It is tall indeed. It has fifty floors, one for each state of the Union, all stacked in alphabetical order with the appropriate state seals on each floor near the elevator. The top floor is Wyoming. This arrangement presupposes that the United States has already fulfilled its manifest destiny. If one of the Southern states secedes, wreckers would presumably withdraw its floor from the Americana. Should Puerto Rico gain statehood, the event would occasion a fifty-first floor, inserted between Pennsylvania and Rhode Island.

As in other new hotels, the most conspicuous service rendered is lip service. An Italian concert singer staying at the hotel was routed from his bed at two A.M. recently

Posh Days on the Potomac

Some awareness of a rising tide of dissatisfaction with the mechanized, non-service hotel is suggested by the efforts of two new establishments in Washington, D.C., to reassure potential patrons. One of them, The Madison (which calls itself "Washington's Correct Address"), has mailed to the general public, as evidence of its determination to emphasize personal service, a bulletin headed "Personal and Confidential to All Employees," in which the following lush passages occur:

"The Madison is the Washington 'town mansion' of its guests, in which each individual is recognized as lord of the manor. . . . The tone of The Madison can best be described as one of *restrained elegance.* . . . Staff members who have direct contact with guests are conservatively dressed in subdued colors; there are no garish uniforms. . . . You [i.e., the employee] will be required to learn the name and title (if any) of every guest, immediately after his or her arrival. Keep in mind that in speaking to guests, the true hotel professional does not say (for example): 'Yes, ma'am' or 'No, sir,' but 'Yes, Mrs. Brown' or 'No, Dr. White.'. . . Desk Managers and Bellmen of The Madison almost never speak of them as, for example, 'those people in 1209.' Instead, guests are spoken of by name, as 'Dr. and Mrs. White,' or 'Mr. and Mrs. Smith.'. . . Desk Managers have always before them a 'history file' [which] contains detailed individual preferences in accommodations and conveniences. No person who has once been a guest of The Madison is ever again a 'stranger' to the staff. . . . Every bathroom has a full length marble vanity, a bathtub five-and-a-half feet long and an RCA ice cube maker."

And from The Georgetown Inn, also in Washington, comes this note in simulated handwriting:

"Dear Mesdames et Messeieurs [*sic*]

"My name is Elijah. I am a butler at The Georgetown Inn. I know more about getting things done in Washington than most legislators, members of the Executive Branch, and the Diplomatic Corp [*sic*].

"For example, if you were a guest at the Georgetown Inn, I would pack and unpack your bags . . . get your theatre and transportation tickets . . . arrange your personal appointment schedule . . . get any message or letter translated in any language including Esperanto. My manners are impeccable, my service gracious, my demeanor most reassuring. I am dedicated to your comfort.

"Won't you give me the pleasure of serving you?

"Sincerely

"Elijah"

by a call from the front desk announcing the arrival of a telegram. The victim asked that the telegram be sent up to his room. When the telegram was still on its way up an hour later, the singer descended to make inquiries. The desk clerk mumbled that there had been a mistake.

Opening-day breakdowns and confusion in the early stages of operation are not of course confined to hotels. They afflict ocean liners and even governments. When a hotel's shakedown cruise lasts for months, however, the management might consider a tactic adopted by apartment builders: Why not offer rent concessions until the place works properly?

In the Americana's La Ronde Café the menus read as though written by ad agencies. Thus, the salads include a "Gay Nineties Chicken Salad," a "Gentleman Jim," and a "South Pacific" (which suggests either fruit or shredded anopheles mosquitoes on a bed of cinchona bark). Desserts are not desserts but "The Sweet Temptations."

Architecturally, the Americana is no temptation. It looks like a bent block. Rooms facing north look out on the new Hilton hotel, whose architecture was inspired by a straight block—the United Nations Secretariat building. The Hilton will have nicer public rooms than the U.N., but fewer public stenographers. Both the Americana and the Hilton have sprung up in a forest of new and almost identical skyscrapers in the vicinity of Sixth Avenue and Fifty-third Street, half of them looking like boxes that the other half came in.

It is too early to judge the quality of service at the Hilton, which will have its formal opening this spring, but certain assumptions can be made about style. The hotel has forty-six floors, one for each of the forty-six states of the Union. Its windows are tinted a blue that the Hilton people have dubbed Hilton Blue, as distinct from Grolier Gold, Seagram Bronze, and Lever Green.

*A*ll 2,153 of the Hilton's rooms have television, radio, and ice-cube units which, according to a news release, "will freeze new cubes as quickly as guests can use them," bonny little cubes that will "set a new trend in hotel operation by eliminating irritating waits for waiter delivery of ice." Sketches reveal the rooms to be furnished with those brass-necked giraffe lamps, those square faceless chests "with a Formica or mar-proof top," those noncommittal sofas that will eventually keep Salvation Army clients in touch with contemporary furniture design. The ice-cube maker will be found in the bathroom wall, as part of a cabinet "incorporated in an overhead light, a medicine chest, a shelf for towels, an automatic tissue-dispenser, an electric outlet, a bottle opener, and a removable magnetic razor-blade disposal container." There is no built-in dishwasher.

"Hospitality Suites" have been named after creative folk like Lorenz Hart, Don Marquis, Damon Runyon, Robert Benchley, O. Henry, and Scott Fitzgerald, and "in décor and theme they symbolize the writings" of these men. A Don Marquis Suite with crumpled copy paper all over the floor and cockroaches on the furniture? For those unluckily susceptible to assassination there is also the Green Room, described as "a maximum security suite for VIP's."

Press agents for the hotel actually boast that frozen foods will be used in the restaurants. There is an electronic wake-up system and electronic computers for totaling bills at the check-out counter. There is an electronic conveyer belt for coats and hats but no electronic shoe-polisher or bedcover turner-backer.

In line with our modern inn-keeping practices and the feverish competition with motels, many new hotels are geared (to use the appropriate figure) to the needs of the motorist, but few of them have attained the advanced design of the projected San Francisco Hilton. That caravansary, when completed, will be enveloped in a spiral "wrap-around garage" enabling the motorist to drive up a ramp to the level of his floor, park his car, enter the hotel through a fireproof door, and go directly to his room through a fireproof corridor, without exposing himself to the other guests, the hotel staff, or outbreaks of smoke and flame for an unnecessary instant. Only one detail must still be worked out: how to get the motorist into his hotel room without making him leave his car.

Whatever line of demarcation there used to be between hotel and motel is now blurred. Urban motels are called motor inns, and they may scrape the sky with as many as twenty floors. It is no mean feat to get a car up to that altitude. Motor inns, or motor hotels, perpetuate the motel tradition by reducing service to compensate for free parking.

New York's tallest, the twenty-story Sheraton Motor Inn, overlooks what its brochures call the "majestic Hudson River" at Forty-second Street. Its own majesty is of the modern variety, nearly identical at first glance to the majestic United Parcel Service garage one block to the north. Ice-cube machines are stationed on every floor. Halls are lit dazzlingly with fluorescent light, as in a set for Sartre's *No Exit.* The elevators are "Autotronic," and consequently vulnerable to attack from little kiddies who like to push all the buttons and make the cars stop at every floor.

From the higher floors the view of the Hudson River piers and ocean liners is truly superb, but the interior views are less invigorating. You rarely feel at home in a motel. You don't feel utterly displaced, either, provided you have stayed at other motels throughout the country and made the acquaintance of the nearly identical brass, plastic, and nylon furnishings. In common with the new hotels, the flossier motel food is escalated Howard Johnson's—with the possible exception of the chain of Howard Johnson motels now proliferating in town and country.

This type of new hotel is not confined to the United States. America may be the fountainhead for slovenly new hotel ideas, but the ideas take root and often flourish abroad, where hotel people make an effort to offer the sort of service, or non-service, they think American tourists demand. An American executive who recently stayed at the new Hilton hotel in Madrid ordered dinner sent up to his suite, then watched a table rolled in with all the components of the meal stacked up and left unset. The waiter deposited this dinner kit and departed, never to return. When the lodger lodged a protest by telephone, a captain arrived on the scene, bowed, and explained that the management thought Americans preferred self-service.

*P*erhaps the most extreme version of the new hotels came into being years before the Americana, the Summit, or the various Hiltons were even on the drawing boards. It was in Stockholm, where the residents referred to it as the "mechanical hotel." There was no help at all, only push buttons. One guest checked out after the automatic shoe-shining machine in the corridor daubed black polish on his new handmade English shoes and turned them from tan to green.

For some years now the Hôtel du Rhône in Geneva has been a glossy outpost of super-Americanism, with its quick lunches and its glassy factory façade. Motels are popping up in many parts of Western Europe and struggling to emulate American methods by eliminating superfluous personal services and substituting a tiny bar of soap or a complimentary shoe-shine rag. The repertoire of American-bred gadgets they can draw from is virtually limitless. In one New Jersey establishment, for instance, the coin box for an unseen slot machine is placed alongside each bed with no clue to its purpose, apparently installed on the assumption that guests will avail themselves of all mechanization. A quarter inserted in the slot provides a few minutes of vibration under the bed, a function performed equally well by trucks on the highway outside.

In another hotel in Los Angeles, a recent "guest-pleasing innovation is the instant-coffee maker . . . equipped with cups, saucers, spoons, and packages of instant coffee, powdered milk and sugar," something of a retreat from the machinery in the Automat, where the milk and coffee are fresh. "When a button is pressed, the machine prepares boiling water; a red light signals when it is ready, and a guest can make himself coffee in a matter of seconds, at any hour of the day or night, or while waiting for room service." The announcement does not specify how many cups of coffee will have been consumed before room service arrives.

The onslaught of automaticity has been relentless. Yet it can be taken as a hopeful sign that the call buttons on the most modern self-service hotel elevators will not respond to any amount of pressure from pencils, nail files, umbrella tips, or gloves. They can be actuated only by the warmth of a human touch.

Joseph Morgenstern, a hotel votary, writes on films and theatre for the New York Herald Tribune.

HairDo Magazine   *HairDo Magazine*

A Theory of the Coiffured Lasses

There came a time, this past fall (see photographs at left), when the fashionable female hairdo seemed headed for the upper limits of verticality and whimsey. The fad passed, and most women went on (as they had all along) cutting and combing to a less extravagant model. Brooding on this phenomenon, the Italian-born cartoonist Marcello Mariotti has produced the chart below, tracing the coiffure from the cave woman to the cub-scout den mother. Will the cycle repeat itself? Like skirt hems and necklines, the headdress can only go up or down so far, and must in theory alternate unto eternity between the two extremes. This theory is available in matching colors and should be washed frequently, even if then you can't do a thing with it.

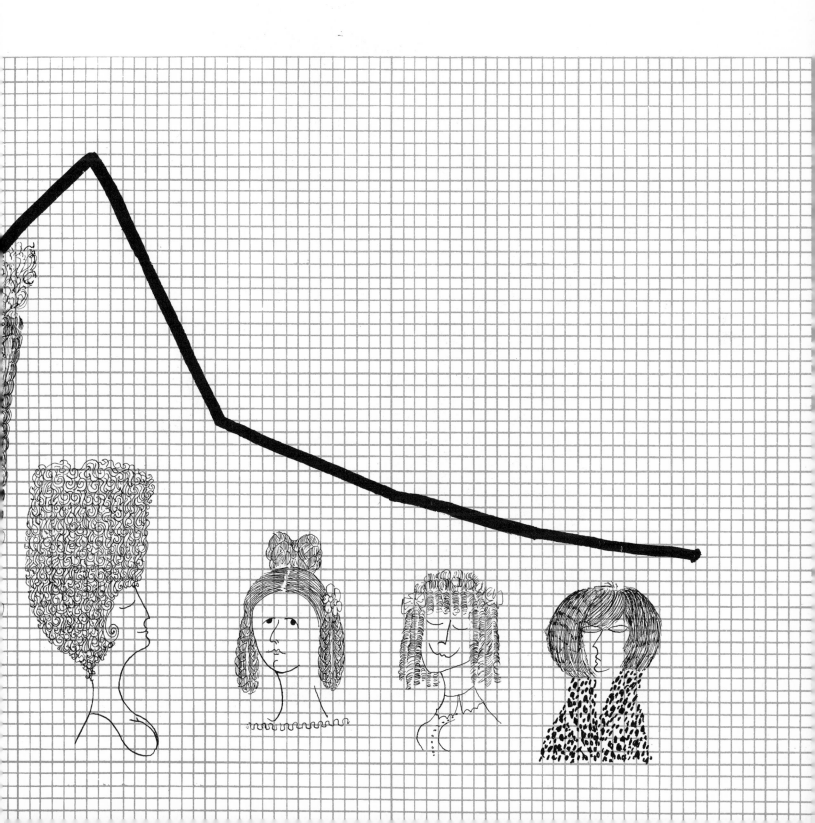

Seal Oil and Soapstone, and the robust folklore of Hudson Bay's Eskimos, are the abundant but hitherto untapped raw materials of art in a land where life is often hard and uncertain. Now, through the efforts of the Canadian government, an Eskimo artist like Natsivaar—whose stone-cut *Angels in the Moon* hover below—can find himself winter work and a wider audience.